ENJOY THE RIDE

REFLECTIONS AND EXERCISES TO GET TO **KNOW YOURSELF BETTER, MAKE CONSCIOUS DECISIONS,** AND **ENJOY THE JOURNEY** TO YOUR DREAMS.

DIOGO SEIXAS

For more information, email diogoseixas91@gmail.com

ISBN: 978-0-578-80565-8

Cover design by 100Covers
Interior design by FormattedBooks

THIS IS JUST THE BEGINNING

First of all, I think it is awesome that you are here. I appreciate you picking up this book and being willing to learn more about who you are and where you want to go. I hope you have a good time with the exercises and reflections in this book, just like I did.

To get the best experience out of this book, I created a workbook for you to print or use online. You will find all the exercises and reflections there as well as in this book. That way, you can keep a personal record of the exercises or redo them anytime you need.

You can get a copy by scanning the QR code or by visiting: www.rideacad.com/resources

Table of Contents

Introduction

Everybody is trying to figure out life, no matter what age they may be. We all struggle with something: habits, emotions, experiences, beliefs, criticism, dreams, values, fear, future, failure, shame, you name it. Personally, I am on the constant lookout to discover who I am, what I like, what I want to do, and where I want to go. I am always searching for ways to be a better person, to be more happy, have better relationships and help more people. Oftentimes, our ambitions seem so big or so complicated, and it seems like we will have to learn and do so many things to achieve them. This can be overwhelming and lead us to think we have absolutely no idea where to start.

Now, if you are older and have some years on your backpack, life has probably taught you some things about who you are. Even so, you probably don't feel like you have learned enough. If you are younger, this need and pressure to figure your life out is huge, and you probably live life day in and day out wondering how on earth you're going to do it. Sometimes, we may know something is wrong in our lives but not know what or why, sometimes we just know something can be better. It's almost as if we are spending our time looking for answers to questions that we don't even know how to formulate.

I believe this unknowing is a growing pain we have that never actually goes away. We are always dealing with existential crises because we have answers to so little. I have experienced them, you have experienced them, and the chances are that we will continue to do so throughout our lives.

The main problem we keep having is that we don't know where to find the answers we are looking for, so we keep running around and getting things done—things that do not relate to our overall vision for life. If you think about it, we've been doing things for our entire lives simply because other people told us to do them. People tell us that we should be rich, and to be rich we should study hard and go to college to get a good career. They say we should be dedicated and fight for what we want. While these are all great things, there comes a point in our lives where we want (and need) to take control of the decisions that can change our course. We need to be the ones making decisions about what we like, where we go, and ultimately who we are and who we want to be. We need to know how to deal with our freaking problems, and how to handle our lives by making our own decisions. We want and need to be better, not because someone told us we must be, but because we want that for ourselves.

I've been on this journey of self-discovery for years now, and I had to find the answers to many of those questions myself. I had to learn how to be more motivated, how to change habits, how to deal with emotions, how to find a future, how to deal with failure, how to find a purpose, how to create goals, how to be happier, and much more. For a long time I thought I was alone, that I was the only weirdo who was lost and trying to figure out his life. I always wanted to make sure I was on the right path before taking the next step, but realized this is not always possible and that is okay. Little by little, I found the answers I was looking for and ended up finding a fulfilling career.

Since 2016, I've worked in the realms of leadership and self-development. I along with some others founded Journey Movement (Movimento Journey in Portuguese) and helped to develop over 4,000 thousand people through speeches and workshops. In 2017, I moved to the United States and started working as the coordinator of the Leadership Development Program (LDP) in Carbondale, Illinois. Over three years, I coached 100 students who had many of the same questions about life. Along this path of leadership and self-awareness, I met many people who, like me, were trying to figure out their lives and felt as lost just as I was—or still am.

That first year in the United States is when I created the Dream Lab, which was a 10-week training where I would guide people through different exercises in the hopes that by the end, they could answer some of the questions they had about this life. The goal of the Dream Lab was never to help students find their dreams, but rather to teach them how to live on the path toward their dreams in the best way possible. Dreams themselves are not concrete; they can and will always change. The journey to a dream, however, is only one, and the more you know about yourself, the better that journey can be.

With the Dream Lab, I wanted to teach people how to stop and evaluate their lives before moving forward. I wanted to teach them how to assess the way in which their lives were and are flowing, and then decide for themselves what they want to do, where they want to go, and who they want to be. I wanted to give people a self-development guide. The Dream Lab taught people how to take a break, breathe, and decide before taking the next step. As one of my students, Madeleine Meyer said, "Before the Dream Lab, I would freak out about everything. I would run around like a chicken with its head cut off. But now, I understand the importance of taking a step back and analyzing the situation, and how to learn and grow from it."

This book is an evolution of the Dream Lab. It is a practical guide with reflections, exercises, and stories about how to do something about "that thing" that has been bothering you. The book itself will not solve all your problems, but if you learn and apply the lessons here, I know it will make the journey to your dreams smoother, happier, and more fulfilling. The coolest thing (I think) about this book is that it's atemporal, meaning that you can—and should—redo those exercises whenever you feel the need.

I believe this book can increase your levels of happiness, motivation, sense of direction, control of life, abundance, and harmony. I want you to be happy about your life but never satisfied with it, always looking for ways to improve. More importantly, I want you to enjoy the ride to your dreams, whatever they might evolve to become. I want you to stop, reflect, and decide consciously what you are going to do next for yourself. I want you to be less anxious and lost about what is about to come.

Like Paul Dolan says in his book, *Happiness by Design,* "Future happiness can't be compensated by the present unhappiness; happiness lost today is happiness lost forever." Right here and now, I'm inviting you on a journey of self-discovery where *you* are in control of the decisions you make. I'll give you the reflection and exercises, and you will find that you have had the answers to your questions all along; you've just been looking in the wrong places.

Are you ready for that?

CHAPTER 01

How This All Began

Let's start from the beginning

Right at the beginning of college, a friend came to me with the idea of opening an AIESEC branch. I had no idea what that was. I remember this friend saying something about helping local communities by making the connection between them and volunteers from all over the world. He said we would bring people to our city to do social work, and send people out to do the same. I had never thought that 21-year-old kids would be capable of doing such a thing, but we did it.

AIESEC is a non-governmental and not-for-profit organization entirely run by students. Founded in 1948 after World War 2, the organization had the dream to build a more united and multicultural consciousness around the world. The acronym, which is no longer used, means the Association Internationale des Étudiants en Sciences Économiques et Commerciales. With branches in 114 countries around the world, the organization provides 30,000 leadership experiences every year for students through social and in-company internships.

AIESEC was the kickoff to all of my other experiences; it was life-changing. I was the president of the local branch for a little over a year, and in that time, I learned a lot about leadership (what to do, and what NOT to do), management, people, marketing, finances, and a bunch more. I made many mistakes, but that only accelerated the learning process.

At one of the local AIESEC conferences, I heard a story that has stuck in my mind ever since. The president of another AIESEC branch talked about an exchange student who came to work for an organization that helps people who are blind. This student from Egypt worked with the organization for six weeks, and on his last day he asked to take a picture with the people he had helped and the staff of the organization. After they finished taking the picture, one of the people he worked with who is blind said this to him:

"It's been so long since someone asked me to take a picture. Thank you for reminding me that I exist."

I can remember vividly the moment when I heard this story for the first time. I remember the goosebumps I felt on my skin and the urge I felt inside me to do something about the message. At that moment, I realized what my calling was for this life. I decided that I wanted to help more people know they exist. I wanted more people to feel like they mattered and that they were important to the world. There was only one question left: How?

A bit before my term was over in the AIESEC, I applied to a government program to study abroad in the United States for one year. I got the news months later that I had been accepted at Southern Illinois University of Carbondale, in Illinois. In June of 2014, I started a journey that was one of the best experiences I've ever had. During my time at SIU, I met many dear friends who changed my life and helped me to become the person I am today. I was a member of the Leadership Development Program, which is an organization that was started in 2007 to enhance the student experience while in college and give them a jump start in their careers after they left.

I remember leaving the first meeting of the Leadership Development Program and talking to my friends about how cool the experience was. My one year as a member of the program helped me realize what true leadership is, how to effectively lead people, and most importantly, that leadership was about practice. Looking back to my time in Brazil, our leadership was very bad. The political scenario was awful and people were losing hope. Thinking about this allowed me to make the connection between that old calling from AIESEC and the experience I was now having in the U.S.: What if people started practicing leadership now? Would it help them be better leaders in the future, would it help them do stuff that matters and consequently change the reality in places like Brazil? Why not in the rest of the world?

A little before the program in the U.S. was over and we had to return home, a few other Brazilians and I decided to start something to change our reality. It took months and months of planning before our first opportunity came—an invitation from Felipe's professor to do a workshop in Cariacica, Espírito Santo in Brazil. In this workshop, we facilitated a training for 30 people and taught about the five leadership practices we had learned in the Leadership Development Program. I remember our attendees leaving that room feeling like they needed to change and to do something different in their lives, and I felt transformed as well.

That day was a tipping point for me. I told my friends that I was going to start an organization to teach people around Brazil about leadership, and that they were more than welcome to join me. In January of 2016, Jean, Felipe, and I started Journey Movement, an organization that believed in leaders who transform their dreams into reality. We did this by teaching leadership practices through training, speeches, and online content.

Everything started with the idea of teaching leadership, making people better, and creating a better world in consequence. In the first six months of Journey Movement's existence, we did four or five training sessions, mostly through connections from friends who believed in our cause. For us, knowing there were people out there who believed in what we do and wanted us to talk about it was surreal.

Since I started on this path, I have become obsessed with learning. I believe that the more I learn, the more I can teach and help others. Since I was broke and never able to afford any expensive training, I turned to free resources, and learned something every spare minute I had from books, podcasts, and videos.

One day I was listening to an interview from Sofia Esteves, CEO of Cia de Talentos, a talent hunting company in Brazil. The social climate in Brazil had gotten very bad; the country was experiencing a crisis. As a consequence, job opportunities were very scarce. When asked about the job market, Sofia said that even though jobs were scarce, they still could not fill all the employment positions available. I thought this was extremely impressive, since many of my friends back home were searching unsuccessfully for work. In doing some further research I found that more than 40,000 engineers and 80,000 business students graduate per year in Brazil. Yet, we can't fill all the job positions available? How is that possible? There are so many people looking for work and so many spots open. Sofia said the problem wasn't in the numbers, the problem was that applicants couldn't answer a simple question: What is your dream?

Now for me, dreaming was always pretty easy. When I was little, I used to imagine my Power Ranger friends and the Teenage Mutant Ninja Turtles fighting side by side with me to take down some kind of monster. I remember getting a little older, dreaming about becoming a soccer player and playing for the national team someday. A little before college, I remember dreaming about my first job and what I was going to do with the money I would make. I dreamed about my family and the vacations we would take together. To me, it seemed so easy to dream; I did it all of the time. I wondered then, why couldn't other people answer Sofia's interview question by defining their dreams?

In 2017, I met Caio Dib in Brazil. Caio has been working tirelessly over the years to learn more about education and to improve the Brazilian system. When I met him, he told me a story he had heard on a TED talk, one where the message was something he had experienced himself as well. He told me about someone who went to a kindergarten class and asked: "Who here wants to be an artist?" All of the kids in the class raised their hands, super excited about this creative notion. Then, the person went into a first grade class and asked the same question. This time, only about 80% of the kids raised their hands. In each higher-level grade that was visited, the number of children who wanted to be an artist got lower and lower until, in a class full of high school seniors, only one person raised their hand.

After hearing this story, I made the connection between it and Sofia's question. We are born dreamers, but with time we lose our sense of creativity and imagination. We get used to people telling us what to do and where to go. Someone else chooses the content we have to learn in school, the classes we need to take to graduate, and what we are going to do with all the information we gain. We learn that we need to be smart to get into college. We then go to college so we can get a good job. We get our good jobs to make good money, because we need that money to afford our family and to buy things for ourselves. Generation to generation, the cycle repeats.

I decided to do my own research about this issue. During my speeches and trainings I started telling people this story of the schoolchildren and asking attendees about their own dreams. I heard so many cool things, so many incredible aspirations. People told me they wanted to become doctors to cure cancer, professors to change the educational system, and politicians to eradicate poverty and misery. Aren't those all awesome goals? Unfortunately, I only heard things like that from maybe 10% of the people I met. The other 90% were people who "didn't have a dream," or if they did, it would be something like, "I want to be successful," or "I want to be rich!" They stuck to safety by giving solely "acceptable" answers.

Don't get me wrong. It's okay to want money, to want success. But those things can't be the final goals. There has to be more, right? Think about your children; would you like them to spend their lives only chasing money? I bet you wouldn't. You'd want them to be happy. You'd probably think that if they could make money while doing what makes them happy, that's even better! All I am saying here (and this has been proven by research, by the way), is that people who chase more than just money are happier. Knowing this, our task is to then discover what "more than money" actually means.

After more than a year of going to different schools and speaking for organizations about the importance of having a dream, I still wasn't happy about the trend away from creativity. I was giving people the "why" it was important to have a dream, but I wasn't giving them the "how" to create one.

In 2017, Dr. DeRuntz, the Director of the Leadership Development Program (the same I had graduated from in 2015), invited me to come back to the United States and work with them, coaching and mentoring students. I thought a lot about whether to take this opportunity, but eventually decided to go. Journey was doing well in Brazil and we were helping a lot of people, but I knew the Leadership Development Program would be a once in a lifetime opportunity. I also knew that everything I would learn in the U.S. with the leadership program and my MBA would exponentiate my impact later on. So in August of 2017, I started my new job as the LDP coordinator and began as an MBA student at Southern Illinois University. At the same time, I was handling things in Brazil with Journey, creating way more content online, and supporting our team's efforts to continue impacting people through speeches and workshops.

Once I got to know my new students at SIU, I started to talk with them about my findings in Brazil regarding dreams and discovered that many of these college kids were having similar identity issues. They were all at a university but still had very few ideas about why, besides to getting a degree. That realization was my call to action: two different countries, two different realities, and still no dreams. I had to do something to change this.

I was shocked that there were still so many people coming out of high school with no ideas about what they wanted to do with their lives. Even now, I would dare say (without any data) that many people in college and even working for big companies don't know what they really want to do with their lives yet, either. Lots of people are just going through life achieving goals without thinking about the directions they want to go. I felt a need to help these people decide that dreams were important and realize the limitless possibilities of life.

To try and combat the major problems I was seeing, I started designing what I called the Dream Lab in late 2017. The Dream Lab is a methodology with practices, exercises, and reflections with the goal of helping people find clarity about their careers and what is coming next. The lab put people through different "experiments" to see what worked and what didn't work in their lives. I created classes where people could get clear about their life experiences, emotions, purpose, role models, goals, and values.

With time, I realized that the Dream Lab wasn't so much about the "big dream," but about the journey one must take to get there. Some of my students left the Dream Lab without knowing what their big dream was, but they knew what their next steps would be to get closer to it. They also had many new tools, exercises, and reflections to use along the way. Watching students go through the Dream Lab made me realize that even when we chase our big dreams, they will change some day, or we will achieve them and find more. Therefore, my goal as I went forward with the Lab wasn't just to help people find their "final destination," but to live their best lives possible. Over the years, the course evolved to the book you are holding in your hands right now.

> **Think about it.**
> Have you ever written your own story? Take some time now and try to write about your life. You will be surprised to reflect on how much you've done and you might actually be proud of how far you've come! This is a great exercise to get to know yourself better and great practice for when you need to introduce yourself to others.

Let's talk about dreams

To get started, here is one of the first and most important things you need to know when reading this book: When I talk about dreams, I'm talking about life, career, relationship, or any other goals that people have for themselves. I know these imagined goals are important for you, because for anything to happen in the real world (for anyone), it first needs to happen inside your head. We all need to dream, to imagine, and to find ways to explore the possibilities of what hasn't yet happened.

Dreams are crucial to living our lives to the fullest, but somehow, over the years, we have lost our creativity. There are several reasons for this, but the biggest one is because we stopped making our own decisions. As we get older, someone is always there to make decisions for us: our family, teachers at school, our society and culture, our friends, etc. We are born dreamers, but we later unlearn how to own that identity because we are taught to "be realistic." We are told that giving up a dream to follow the "safer" or "easier" path is a better long-term choice.

You saw so many people doing this too, right? I know I did growing up. I saw family and friends making sensible decisions about their lives all the time despite wanting something else, and we see this so often that we end up believing the realistic choices really are best. Because this is what we see, we might have given up on our own dreams too, meaning that we have contributed to the culture of not dreaming.

When someone gives up their dream to follow the "normal" path, they are teaching other people around them to do the same. Little by little, we see our friends giving up, maybe someone in our family giving up, and in the future, that's what we are going to be teaching our kids and grandkids. Is that really the kind of world we want to create? One where the realistic path is always the right path? One where we "do what we gotta do" and not what we love to do?

I'm willing to bet that just about every dream you have heard of, no matter how many people thought it was too crazy, was something that would make the world a better place. The professor, the doctor, the politician... If those people had pursued their dreams, think about the world they could build together. Think about how much positivity and impact they would've caused. We don't just need more people like Bill Gates, Steve Jobs, and Madre Theresas, we need more people like you. You are important. I am important. We are all important. Everybody has something to contribute to the world. In his book, *The Alchemist*, Paulo Coelho says, "No matter what he does, every person on earth plays a central role in the story of the world. And normally he doesn't know it."

Maybe at this point you are starting to think that this is just another one of those motivational books—more bla bla

bla about the power of following our dreams and being happy. And if you think like this, maybe you have been tricked into the culture of not dreaming. Maybe you tried something once or twice, or even many times, but it didn't work and you decided to blame the world for it. Maybe you have never tried anything, but you learned through the experiences of someone else that dreaming was a waste of time and never challenged that belief. If you think this is BS and don't do anything to change that limiting belief, you are a part of (and a perpetuator of) the culture of not dreaming.

To be honest, I really don't care what you believe. However, I do know you believe that if all dreams came true (like Walt Disney said), we would have a better world. That's what everybody wants, right? We want that person who dreams about being a better politician; we want that person who dreams about curing cancer, about making the educational system better, about solving the world's hunger problem. Isn't that true?

Simply because of the fact that we want a better world for ourselves and those around us, we need to support the dreamers (and have dreams of our own). And please, even if you don't believe in this for yourself, don't get in the way of the people who do. If you see someone dreaming high, give them stronger wings. Incentivize them, support them. Or maybe, just be quiet. But never, never, ever clip what can allow someone to soar. It's like the saying, "If you are not going to help, don't get in the way."

To expand on this a little more, at this link there is a five-minute long talk I gave on the importance of dreaming at an event called Ignite Talks. You can access the video by

scanning the QR code on the right or going to our website https://www.rideacad.com/

I'm here to ask you to, before anything else, incentivize the culture of dreaming. Dream yourself, and cultivate an environment that helps other people dream as well. We all want a better world, and I truly believe that this is the first step. I believe that if we can dream more and support one another, we can create a culture of positive change that will make us happier.

The only thing that might get in your way

I hope that by now, you are thinking about joining the movement and becoming a dreamer. At the same time, I acknowledge that you might have a thousand different things running through your brain: Am I good enough? Am I on the right path? Do I have what it takes? What if I fail?

It's okay to think about these things; they still come up for me on occasion too. It's all part of the process. At the same time, self-doubt is not the biggest problem dreamers face.

The biggest problem for dreamers is anxiety. We want things to happen fast and we don't want to make any mistakes. For a second, I want you to think about a house that has been built brick by brick. If we rush the process because we want it to be finished quickly, we run the risk of forgetting a single, yet extremely crucial brick. Guess what happens when someone forgets one brick? The whole house collapses.

The same thing happens with our lives, careers, relationships, etc. Even though we might have a clear picture of what we want things to look like, if we build them in a rush, we might forget a critical component and risk having everything fall apart. This could mean building the right future with the wrong person, your career without a purpose, or your life with no happiness.

We need to understand that the process of becoming a dreamer and building the futures we want is just that—a process—and when we skip part of the process, the product at the end won't be what we hoped. Therefore, chill. Life will happen anyway, and there is no need to rush the process or risk having an undesirable product at the end. Understanding this helps us to be more calm when we do fail, because it's part of the process to creating the best product. I like to think it's better to fail at a small step in the process (when there is still time to change things) than to fail on a large scale at the end of the line.

The Hero's Journey

Think about any traditional hero story for just a minute. It typically starts with a call to some adventure where the hero is excited about what is about to come. In the very beginning, however, he encounters challenges and very often fails. He keeps trying and trying, little by little improving his skills. Finally, one day, the hero gets tested with an even greater challenge than the one he faced at the start, and he fails even worse than before. But he is a hero, so he doesn't give up! He comes back to the challenge, tries even harder, and *finally* achieves success.

Then when he thinks it's all over... he starts again.

The Hero's Journey is a sequence of events which were popularized by Joseph Campbell. Most stories follow this logic; the character goes through ups and downs throughout the whole story until at last, he achieves success in the end.

Our lives follow the exact same pattern. My favorite parallel to draw from the Hero's Journey is that life is a cycle and it has ups and downs. If you are top right now and have achieved success in something, you should start to get ready for the next challenge that's coming. If you think you hit rock bottom and that life keeps hitting you over and over it's okay, because you are growing from your circumstances and soon, you will overcome your current challenge. There is always something good at the end of the tunnel, but there are always more tunnels. All the effort you are putting in right now will be rewarded, and every cycle of ups and downs gets easier because you can have confidence in knowing you've made it through before.

If life follows the same cycles repeatedly, the secret is learning how to make the best of wherever you are in the cycle at any given time. If we know how to navigate through life in the best way, we can take advantage of how we are living right now. If you can learn how to deal with failure, emotions, anxiety, habits, beliefs, and whatever might get in your way of success, you increase the chances of making the best of this cycle and increasing the quality of your life.

Think about it

Have you ever thought about your life in terms of the Hero's Journey? What are your highs and lows? Which phase would you say you are in right now?

This is my guide of how to do this

For years now, I've been studying self-improvement and have learned so much about the topic. My favorite authors are Brené Brown, Mark Mason, Ken Robinson, Daniel Pink, Anthony Robbins, Murilo Gun, and others. I want to make it clear here that some of the ideas in this book are a combination of ideas from different authors, as well as myself. Murilo Gun, brazilian speaker and creativity professor, always talks about "combinativity" as the fusion of the words "combination" and "creativity." Nothing is created; everything is combined. I believe this is the perfect way to define the book you are currently holding. It is made up of both my best imagination and creativity.

You know when you go into Spotify, Apple Music, or any other music streaming service, and you choose a genre of music that you want to listen to? This book is like a playlist of the self-development genre: it is a collection of lessons, exercises, and reflections that might help you navigate through this beautiful and complicated thing called life.

I have put together all the things I think you should know to make your journey the best possible one it can be. My goal in writing this was not to go in-depth about everything, but to give you an overview of the topics to help you learn more about yourself and your aspirations. After reading this, you will know where to go for more content if you want to continue learning, but more importantly, you will know how to apply these concepts in your own life. I want you to take action and find ways to change what you are not happy about right now. It's up to you to make that happen.

I'm a huge fan of the TV show, *Friends*. At the beginning of the first episode of season one, the group is helping Rachel adapt to her new life in New York City. She was almost married to someone she didn't love, and after an epiphany she fled her wedding and ran into the Central Perk. At the end of this first episode, she cuts her credit cards one by one to symbolize her new life without her parents' money. When the process is complete, Monica says, "Welcome to the real world, it sucks! You're gonna love it!" I make her words mine fairly often. Life is crazy, but it's definitely one of the best things we'll ever have. Let's make the journey the very best it can be.

CHAPTER 02

How To Be Successful In This Book

It's never about the exercise

Throughout this book, we will do different exercises that can help you to think about life and reflect on your experiences, strengths, growth opportunities, dreams, values, and much more. It's important to set expectations for this process because most of the learning will come from the reflections *about the exercise*, not just by doing the exercise. You get what you put in. If you want to have the best possible results, I recommend you spend some time thinking about what you have learned from each set of exercises and how you can start putting that information into action right now. Before we start though, here are a few ground rules that you should follow to have the best experience:

Be clear about the Why

Understand the reasons why you are reading this book. What do you want to learn? What do you want to get out of this experience? Do you want to improve your life? Do you want to change your career? Do you want to get to know yourself better? Do you want to be better? Do you want to be better to someone else? When we are clear about our intentions, the learning process is more powerful because we see meaning behind what we are doing.

> **Think about it**
> Why did you pick up this book? What are your expectations for it? What is the overall goal you hope to achieve by reading it?

Never complete the exercises in a rush

As we talked about earlier, doing things in a rush might cause us to skip important steps of the process. Take your time in doing the exercises. It's not about getting them done, but what can you learn about yourself while doing them. We don't want to waste time or resources, so if you are going to do the exercise, do it well. We are talking about your life here!

Find pleasure doing the exercises

If you can find pleasure in the work, the experience will be even better. I love reading with a cup of coffee or tea in the morning, but I love doing these kinds of exercises—with some music in the background—in the evenings before going to bed. That's when I get the most reflexive about life. Find your best moment to get this done.

<u>Be free of judgments and be curious</u>

When you start an exercise, be curious about what you can learn about yourself. It's a safe life experiment that you are doing right now. Don't expect anything from it, and don't try to predict the conclusions. At the end of every session of the Dream Lab, I asked my students what their a-ha moment was in the session. Oftentimes, the lessons were not even related to the exercise. I bet this will happen with you as well. Just be patient with yourself and try new things to see what will happen.

<u>Think about: What are the three things I learned about myself during this exercise?</u>

As I just mentioned, it is crucial to think about what you have learned about yourself at the end of each exercise. Did anything come up that you were not expecting? Did anything surprise you? It's never about the exercise itself, but about the things you can learn from it. Make some effort at the end of each chapter or exercise to ask yourself these questions.

Think about it

Throughout the book, you will see boxes like this one with little reflections inside. I would recommend that once you reach these boxes, you either take a break from reading to really think about the information you just learned, or save some time at the end of the chapter to reflect on the content in the box.

Find one place to write your reflections

In the next chapter, we will talk about journaling and how this practice can help you to get to know yourself better. Having the exercises and reflections written down in your journal is a great way to keep track of your progress and to understand more about who you are! Consider completing everything in your journal. An alternative option is to use the workbook, which you can print or use on your computer. To access the workbook you can use the website https://www.rideacad.com/resources or scan the QR code on the right.

Our agreement

Before we start, I want to say that I'm extremely proud of you for picking up this book. I've been helping so many people throughout the years in different ways and I love to see how much they change during our time together. Hopefully, we will have the same experience with this book, and somehow I'll help you as well.

I promise you that I gave my best in creating this guide, trying to summarize everything I have learned and break it down into actionable steps so you can apply them in your life. What I need from you now is commitment—to put aside a few minutes of your week to read these pages and think about the exercises. The cool thing about this book is that it has a different answer for each person's questions. Depending on where you are in your life, you will gain different pieces of insight. I hope I can guide you well toward the answers you need.

Have fun :)

CHAPTER 03

How To Do Journaling

How much do you know about yourself?

We will start this chapter with some quick math. (Sorry if you are not a fan; I'll try to make this as painless as possible.) Have you ever thought about how much time you spent in school? Usually, we have about 16 weeks per semester, so that's a total of 32 weeks of classes per year. Let's say that, on average, we spend eight hours a day in school (if we count classes and homework). This means we spend 40 hours a week in school (not including any weekend work). Multiplying the hours per week by the weeks per year, we spend a total of 1,280 hours in school per year.

Now we add in the variable that makes things different for everybody, depending on where they are in their educational journey. If you completed high school, you had 13 years of formal education, which means you spent 16,640 hours inside a classroom. If you completed college, you spent an extra four years—if everything went "right"—in the system, which added another 5,120 hours to your running total of 21,760 hours of school education. If you are still in college, it means that you have spent somewhere between 1.90 and 2.48 years straight, day and night, inside a classroom.

You have spent so much time learning about math, languages, science, and humanities, plus the more field-specific information you learned through the career path you chose. This is all great! But I have a question for you: How many hours have you spent learning about yourself? How much time did you spend thinking about your future, about what you want to do or the path you want to take? How much did you learn about your emotions and habits? How much do you actually know today about who you are?

When thinking about my own education, I don't really remember my professors talking about those kinds of things in the classroom. I do remember some of them giving pieces of advice about life, but I can't remember what that advice was, either. In high school, speakers from outside came to talk about skills we should have, like how to study better and faster. Parents also came in to talk about their profession in the hopes of inspiring students.

The truth is that we don't learn much about who we are in school. I even joke around sometimes by saying I learned in school everything that I *didn't* want to do in life. I know this might sound harsh, but most of who I am today comes from the things I did outside the classroom. School is great to give you tools you can use in the workforce, but it's common knowledge that it doesn't give you much guidance to help you figure out who you are. It's kind of the assumption they have when you come to school, that you should already know your life's path. When school professionals do give attention toward self-discovery in class, it is not nearly enough to serve all the students to the best extent possible.

I bet that if schools spent more time helping students to figure out who they are, they wouldn't just have happier students, they would also have more successful students who grew to thrive in careers they truly wanted. Just to be clear, I'm not saying there aren't schools out there investing in this area of education, because there are. If you want to know more about schools like this, you can read books like, *Creative Schools: The Grassroots Revolution That's Transforming Education,* by Ken Robinson and *The One World Schoolhouse: Education Reimagined,* by Salman Khan.

Unfortunately, the majority of schools still run with the traditional system in place, and it's up to us to find for ourselves where we want to go and who we want to be. In his book, *You, Your Child, and School: Navigate Your Way to the Best Education*, Ken Robinson discusses a time where he was talking with a group of students and one of them said, "Some of our professors are really boring. What can we do about that?" Robinson said, "You can't put this all on your teachers. If you are bored, that's something to do with you, too. You shouldn't just sit in front of the teacher and think, 'Well, go on, interest me.' It's your education. Get interested and take responsibility." I love this passage because it reminds us that we have responsibility and control over our situations. It's easy to sit down and complain about everything that is wrong in our lives, but not many people take responsibility for those things and focus on making change.

I truly believe that if people spent just 1% of their time reflecting about their lives and their next steps, 99% of their problems would be solved. I'm going to use some math here again really quickly. One percent of our time represents 14 minutes and 24 seconds of our day.

Of those 21,760 hours of education that have been completed after you graduate college, you would've spent 217.6 hours learning about you if you set aside 1% of your time. That's only nine straight days, instead of 2.48 years in school. In my mind, it's a very small price to pay so that you can be more clear about who you are and what you want to do. The good news is that even if you have not started there is still hope, and taking responsibility for your education is the first and most important step.

Think about it
Think about how much you have invested in yourself over time. Think about this both in terms of time and money. You are a valuable asset, and the more you invest in yourself, the more you get from the experience of life. How does that notion relate to where you are in life right now?

When did you become a grown up?

I don't remember when this curiosity started, but for a while now I've been wondering about when people became grown ups. When I was little, I saw my cousins coming back from high school and it felt like they were so smart and mature, getting ready for the life that was about to happen for them. Then, when I got to high school years down the road, I didn't feel the way I thought it would feel to be so "grown." It seemed like I was the same kid I always was, just a few years older. I thought maybe college was when everything would change and I would feel like a grown up, but when I got there and was living by myself, I felt like I still wasn't there. I was just starting to figure everything out, not even close to knowing all there was to know. Next, I assumed that when I got my first job and started to live without my parents' help, I would feel more grown up. Nope. Today I live by myself, make my own money, have a bachelor's and a master's degree, and still feel like something is missing. Maybe the next step is to have a family or kids?

As always, I asked this question to other people. I asked my friends on social media to see when they became adults, if they felt like they had. I received the widest range of answers possible. One person told me that they realized they became an adult when they used the money they had been saving to party to buy a nonstick pan. Some people said it happened when they started living on their own money and making their own decisions. Some said it was when they got hurt by someone they loved or when they lost someone close to them.

I extended my informal research to friends of friends and strangers as well. I asked the parents of a friend if they thought they were grown ups, and the wife said sometimes she still feels as if she is 18 and dating her now-husband like they did in high school. Yet, everything changes when they get a call from one of their three children asking for or about something. I asked a 70-year-old Uber driver the same question; he laughed in my face and said that he still feels like a teeneger, screwing up everything he does. He said that even parenting is just one screw up after another, and that people become adults after they hit rock bottom and survive to come back from a bad experience.

It's extremely interesting to see the answers from different people about when they became adults. Try to ask your parents and friends about it; you will have a lot of fun! The conclusions I reached with my mini experiment are that there isn't a fixed point that translates to becoming an adult, and honestly, most people are still figuring out what "adulting" actually means. We are all just trying our best.

This is why it is never too late to start learning about yourself. Even if you have spent those 20,000+ educational hours learning nothing about yourself, you can always catch up. There are many ways that you can begin, and hopefully if you invest a good amount of effort and time into the reflections and exercises from this book, I'll help you clarify a bunch of cool things about yourself. Now, if you are ready, there is one very important aspect of the journey that you can start doing today, and it will be an excellent kickoff to your self-discovery.

Think about it

Have you ever thought about this question? When did you become a grown up (if you ever did)? What happened that made you feel like an adult? In addition, what are some of the qualities a non-adult has that you wish you could never lose?

Get a freaking journal!

Think about a computer. Let's say you have had the same computer for quite some time now, and for a while it's been running a little slow. Does it mean it's a bad computer and it's time to throw it away? Probably not. It's a possibility that there are too many different programs processing in the background, and it's making the rest of the software run slowly.

The solution for that particular problem is to shut down some of those programs; then, the computer will start working well again.

The same thing happens in our brains. We are processing so many things all of the time. We are worried about work, friends, relationships, dinner, meetings, feelings, etc. Our brains are working constantly, reflecting on what just happened, trying to find the best way to do what we are doing in the moment, and planning what comes next in the future. No wonder why it is hard to think about the direction we want to go with our lives when we are focused nonstop on getting things done. We need to be able to shut down some of the processing that takes place in the background to be able to focus on ourselves.

There are many ways in which we can shut out some of those background programs by spending that 1% of our time reflecting on life. The best ways for me to focus are when I exercise, when I'm in bed minutes before sleeping, when I am in the shower, when I am talking to myself during random moments of the day and, my personal favorite, when I write things down in my journal.

I've been journaling since 2016, and it definitely changed my life. Since then I have never stopped, and it has become something that has improved me in many ways, as well as the lives of my students and friends to whom I recommended it. Here are some of the reasons why you should always keep a journal:

It takes the ideas out of your head: If all of your problems are floating around in your head, your focus will never be on anything critical. It's also much easier to get overwhelmed when you can't filter anything out. When you take problems and ideas out of your mind and write about them, you open up mental space to start thinking about solutions for those problems.

It helps you to get clear about your feelings: Very often, we get stressed or frustrated about something or someone in our life. If we can write about these situations, it helps us to reflect about and learn from them. The best thing about recording your feelings is that when they happen again, you already know what to do and how to react.

You become more conscious about who you are: We go through life reacting from one thing to the next. When you write things down, you learn more about yourself and start to get clear on some patterns in your life. In this way, you can better understand who you are and make conscious decisions about what you want to change.

You don't forget things: One of the classic tools people use when journaling is the "to do list." Writing down the things you need to do not only makes you more susceptible to remembering them, but it increases the chances of you actually completing them. By writing them down, you are making a commitment to yourself; it's hard to then face the disappointment of inaction.

It makes things happen: This is slightly related to the one above, but just like that, whatever you write down in your journal happens. I journaled about writing a book, and here I am. When I first thought about the Dream Lab, it all started with a note in my journal, reminding me to test my theories and activities with my students. When you write things down, you redirect your conscious and unconscious attention to a central goal. Therefore, every time you see something that might help you reach that goal, your brain is going to get your attention.

It tracks your progress: When you see how many things you've done in the past and how you survived both the good and the bad, it gives you a sense of achievement and progress. Journaling gives you constant feedback about who you are, teaching you what you can do better. Progress generates progress, constantly motivating you to do and want more.

It takes the pressure off of life: When you go back and review your journals, you will realize that what happened in the past was not as bad as you thought it was. This will hopefully take the pressure off of what you are living through now, and possibly extend to the things that you have yet to live. You will learn that many answers in your future will come from past experiences that have been recorded in your journal. You realize, from all you've persevered through, that everything will be okay in the end.

Think about it

Actually, don't think about it. Just act and buy a journal. It will be one of the best investments you have ever made.

How to start a journal

I hope that by now I have convinced you about how important it is to have a journal. The best part about journaling is that there isn't a right or wrong way to do it. My techniques improved with time and became more complex after years of practice.

I found a lot of good ideas for my journaling practice when I read the book, *Dot Journaling—A Practical Guide: How to Start and Keep the Planner, To-Do List, and Diary That'll Actually Help You Get Your Life Together*, by Rachel Wilkerson Miller. In this book, Rachel talks about exercises, types of journals, and even pens that you can use to write your thoughts. For even more ideas, you can follow the hashtag #bulletjournal on social media. Here, you will see tons of people sharing their strategies for how to journal.

As I said before, you can get as fancy as you want with all of this. Some people love colors and special pens. Some love doing intricate letters and well-designed tables to keep track of their habits. I like to be professional and discreet, so I use a black, dotted, hardcover journal and always write with black pen. I won't lie in that I do have my preferences about which pens I use, but it's not like I refuse to write with any other black pens. I like to keep my journal organized so I always have boxes around my topics to separate one from the other. Even though my journaling follows a pattern now, it wasn't always like this. My first one was just a regular notebook where I wrote things down so I wouldn't forget about what I had to do. I regret to say that I threw it out and ended up losing all the information anyways.

Overall, it's up to you to figure out what works best. The most important thing is that the activity needs to be pleasurable. Don't journal because you think you have to. Don't organize because you think you have to. Don't get fancy because you think you have to. You have to figure out what brings you pleasure and move from there. In a bit, I'll tell you some exercises you can start doing to practice journaling, and the idea is that you will try them and see what works best for you. All I can say is that whatever works best will help you a lot, but it's up to you to figure out what that is.

Here are just a few ideas you could try incorporating into your journaling practice:

Be organized: This is something I learned later on in journaling and continue to work on each week I always start my journals with a quote. In my past three journals, I've been using the "Man in the Arena" speech from Theodore Roosevelt to pull from. This is followed by an index I created, so I can easily find things in my journal (this is even more useful when I need to find notes from my previous ones). I always have a few lists in the beginning (like my Dream List, which helps me to never forget about my dreams and goals). At the end of my journal, I have a list of books and values, as well as a blank page that I write the closing note in for each one.

Week review: Every Sunday night or Monday morning I do this exercise to evaluate my week. I write one page about what I did right that week, what I did wrong, and what I will do better next week. This is a great weekly feedback process that you can do to improve. An extra tip here is to do a semester evaluation too; those are always very helpful.

Weekly to-do list: Followed by the weekly review, I create my to-do list. This is where I write the things I need to get done that week. It's useful if you can split it up by topics (for example, work and personal). If you use this, you will not forget things, plus you can track your progress and feel accomplished.

Track progress: Just like using the to-do lists, tracking progress of your behaviors helps you to be more motivated to improve. I track the progress of how many pages I read per week, how many miles I run, how much time I spend on my phone, how many total books I read, etc. You can get as creative as you want with this. The important thing is to think about the new habits you want to implement, and find a way to track your progress.

Review trainings and books: When I finish a book or training, I like to review the content I learned and make some notes. I love to highlight information from books, so in my journal I also write down the book highlights. This is a good way for me to review, re-learn, and remember what I just saw and store that knowledge somewhere outside of my brain. Since you will have an organized and beautiful index in your journal, if you do this you can always go back to that when you need to locate information from a particular resource.

Meeting notes: I always take my journal to meetings and write notes about the discussions that take place. This is an excellent way to keep track of my observations and plan my next steps. Usually, if I have a task to be completed after that meeting, I also make sure I record it on my to-do list.

Ideas, feelings, and reflections: Every time I have an idea, I make sure to write it down so I don't forget it. If you have feelings that are bothering you because of someone or something that happens, don't be afraid to write them down. It's a great way to ponder and reflect. If you are like me and love life reflections, write those down too; they can be very important in other future moments of your life.

A few extra observations

Friends and students whom I have known to journal tell me how much the practice has helped them. One time, my students from the Leadership Development Program and I were playing a "get to know each other" exercise and someone asked, "If your house was about to burn down, what would be the things you would save from it?" Many people said, between other things, that they would save their journals. Once you begin consistently practicing and seeing results from journaling, you gain access to the book of your life. Your journal contains what happened to you in the past and serves as a manual that you can use for the future. You will see that it becomes a very important practice in your life.

In this ever-evolving world of technology, people always ask if they can use their phones or apps like Evernote, Apple Notes, or Microsoft OneNote to create their journals. Honestly, you can do whatever you'd like, but I'll tell you that online apps do not have the same feeling as writing things down on paper. When you write your thoughts on paper they become real; when you type things they are still not part of this world. Besides that, the physical act of writing slows the process of understanding and reflection, which is the whole point of keeping a journal. Typing might be faster or better organized, but the goal is not to do things efficiently. The goal is to reflect and get to know yourself better, and I promise that quickly is not the way to do this.

Another important part of creating a successful journaling practice is that you need to carry your journal with you at all times. I always have mine on top of my work desk when I'm home and in my backpack when I'm away. It's the second thing I take out of my backpack after my notebook, no matter where I am. I carry with me when I'm traveling, when I am in a meeting, listening to a presentation, and even when I'm sitting in class. You never know when you will have an idea, insight, or reflection, so it's very important to have your journal with you as much as you can. As I said, it becomes part of who you are.

Finally, don't forget to find pleasure in journaling. I was doing daily evaluations for some time and it became so boring that I had to stop. When I tried weekly evaluations instead, they worked much better for me. I look forward to doing them now because I am doing them at the right frequency for me. The keys are to pay attention to what you like and what you don't like, and always look for pleasure. If some journaling strategy you are using causes some kind of pain or boredom, stop that one and try to find something different to do.

Exercise - The Dream Journal

Now that you know the benefits of keeping a journal and how to start one of your own, it is up to you to make it happen. I would strongly recommend you get one as soon as possible and start trying some of the exercises proposed above. I would also recommend that you write down the answers from the questions asked in this book there, and take some time to reflect on your progress.

To give you a head start, I recommend the following exercises as well:

On one of the first pages, build your **Big Dreams** list: I always start my journals with this list. You can write down anything you want to do, no timeline involved. You can write down dreams you have for this year and also for the future. I love having this at the beginning of my journal because it not only helps me not to forget about or neglect my big dreams, but there is easy access to it when I think of something different that I want in my life and want to write it down.

On the following pages, build a few more **Bucket** lists: This is a great exercise to practice your reflection skills, and it will also serve as a generator for ideas to put on your Big Dreams list. Use four pages from your journal to write your "I want to" lists. Write down things you want to do, things you want to have, things you want to learn, and things you want to give to others. When writing these four lists, ask yourself if anything sticks out from them as especially crucial. If so, you can transfer those items to your Big Dreams list.

A very important step for both of the exercises above is to set a minimum amount of time per list. I think five minutes is an excellent starting point; it is usually enough to write what is on your mind and to give yourself a few extra minutes to dig deep down for other things you might have never thought of before. It's very important to stretch your reflection a little bit—that's when the craziest and most valuable ideas spring forward. Don't be happy with five items. Go above and beyond for yourself!

Takeaways

⚷— How many hours have you spent learning about yourself? How much time did you spend thinking about your future, about what you want to do or the path you want to take?

⚷— "Get interested and take responsibility." It reminds us that we have responsibility and control over our situations. It's easy to sit down and complain about everything that is wrong in our lives, but not many people take responsibility for those things and focus on making change.

⚷— I truly believe that if people spent just 1% of their time reflecting about their lives and their next steps, 99% of their problems would be solved. One percent of our time represents 14 minutes and 24 seconds of our day.

⚷— That there isn't a fixed point that translates to becoming an adult, and honestly, most people are still figuring out what "adulting" actually means. We are all just trying our best. This is why it is never too late to start learning about yourself.

⚷— We are processing so many things all of the time. Our brains are working constantly, reflecting on what just happened, trying to find the best way to do what we are doing in the moment, and planning what comes next in the future. We need to be able to shut down some of the processing that takes place in the background to be able to focus on ourselves. Journaling is a way to do that.

Journaling needs to be pleasurable. Don't journal because you think you have to. Don't organize because you think you have to. Don't get fancy because you think you have to. You have to figure out what brings you pleasure and move from there.

CHAPTER 04

How To Use Feedback To Improve Yourself

Setting your start point

Once, when moving from one job to another, I decided to ask for feedback from a bunch of people about me. My goal was to have a general perspective of how people perceived me from different areas of my life. I talked to supervisors, my parents, my brother, my friends, my students, and past co-workers. I received feedback from more than 10 different people and having that, I wanted to do two things: reaffirm what I knew about myself with the hopes that it would boost my courage, and look for things that I could improve upon as a person, leader, and educator for others.

Essentially, I asked people two questions: What I was good at, and what could I improve on? It was one of the most amazing experiences I've ever had. I learned how most people saw me as insightful, great at reading people, and excellent at explaining "life stuff." I also learned that sometimes I push my ideas too hard, I get stressed when things don't work the way I want them to, and I should try to have a little more patience. These were all extremely great for me to hear, because I never realized that I was so pushy. I always saw myself as passionate instead, and had no idea that it bothered people. Additionally, I kind of knew that I got very stressed when my ideas were not accepted, but I never thought this was something other people could see.

I can't say how valuable it is to get feedback from people you care about regarding different areas of your life. I know you think that the person you are at work is not the same as the person you are at home, and it shouldn't be, but you would be surprised how many times those two overlap. Getting feedback from different areas of your life helps you to understand who you are and how you act in different scenarios.

Sometimes, who you really are may not be the same as who other people think you are. The actions that show our true selves are often not aligned with how we want other people to see us. Feedback is a great way to balance this, and to make sure that our actions are being seen by other people in the way we want them to be seen. For example, I learned that I can stop feeling like someone is challenging me every time my ideas are not accepted, and that everyone has feelings and needs that need to be accounted for before implementing the ideas I have. I also realized through feedback that I was hiding my potential at that moment of my life and I needed to challenge myself with something bigger. I had no idea people could see these things when they were in contact with me, but knowing that was a huge push for me to start writing this book and to pursue some sleepy dreams I had.

Getting feedback from others is an excellent starting point to understanding who you are and where you stand in front of those who care about you. It's a great way to balance your actions and your thoughts to become the best version of yourself. We are trying to be more conscious about ourselves with the information in this book; with the inputs you receive, you can reaffirm strengths you have and understand parts of yourself that can be improved.

A note about the best version of yourself

It only matters what you think is the best version of yourself. Yes, you. It really doesn't matter what I think, what your family thinks, or what your friends think. The reason why I reiterate this is because lately I've seen a lot of posts circulating about how to become the "best version of yourself," where the authors give you a magic formula for how to become *that person*. The problem with this is that you are unique; you have different goals, aspirations, and values than everyone else. For this reason, we can't have the same formula for everybody and those posts that tell you otherwise will always disappoint.

My meaning for the best version of myself might be totally different than your version for yourself. If you believe the best version of yourself is having an awesome career, great! If it means being the best parent ever, great! If it means having an average job to pay your bills while focusing on taking care of your garden, great! The best version of yourself is what *you* decide, not what other people decide for you.

I remember being at a point in my life where I was crazy about my productivity, working out, eating healthy, making money, and so on. I pushed myself to be *that person* as much as I could. In another point in my life, I was extremely happy with other things: I enjoyed having chill mornings where I could read and learn, productive afternoons where I could write and get my ideas out of my head, and relaxing evenings where I could talk to my friends, girlfriend, and enjoy a TV show.

Think about what the best version of yourself looks like (to you), and then think about how your actions, decisions, and behaviors are helping you to reach that person. The best version of yourself doesn't only define where you are now, but also where you want to go. And always remember, it's your decision, not anyone else's.

Think about it
What does it mean to you to be the best version of yourself?

Feedback is data collection

Think of feedback as a kind of research that you are conducting to improve yourself. In a simplistic way, we need to collect data when doing research, analyze it, make conclusions, and implement the findings. This is a neverending cycle that we can use to get better all the time. Each part of this cycle is extremely important and we are going to work on all of them when it comes to utilizing this exercise.

I want to give feedback a different meaning here, because many people are traumatized by bad experiences they have had with negative feedback in the past. Unfortunately, people don't know how to give or receive feedback, and as a consequence, it becomes a painful process for most people. That's why, before asking for it or giving it to someone else, laying ground rules for feedback is critical.

If you are receiving feedback, it's important to separate the person who is giving it from the words they are saying. It's not a criticism, and you don't need to accept everything they are saying. Your job is to listen and reflect on it, that's all. If you are giving feedback, you are the one setting the rules. When communicating, focus on the behavior of the receiver, how the interaction is making you feel, and the impact your conversation might have on your relationship with the receiver or in your relationships with other people. It's not about what you say, but how you say it. There is a lot of information online and in books for this, so I don't want to go into too much detail here. My goal in this moment is to help you to understand the value of asking for and receiving feedback while on track to become the best version of yourself.

The most crucial aspect to remember is that the feedback you give or receive needs to be used in order for it to have been beneficial. Think about this for a second: feed(it)back. Any input you collect should be at least considered and reflected on before dismissing or implementing. You don't need to agree with all the input you get, but you do need to think about it. Every process needs ongoing improvement; and we are no exception.

We are doing this because, ultimately, we want to be better and become the best version of ourselves possible. We are not getting feedback to shape ourselves into what other people want us to be, but rather to make sure that our actions are aligned with what we want other people to see.

Think about it
If you had to define feedback, how would you do it in a manner that is powerful? Be creative!

Exercise - data collection

This is a process similar to what I ran on my own, and that I think it's one of the most effective ways to do this. We will split this exercise into three parts: data collection, analysis, and implementation. With data collection, you will conduct "interviews" and ask for feedback. For data analysis, you will look at what you have collected and see what you can learn from it. In the third phase, implementation, you will look for actions you can start taking right now to create change.

Data collection

For data collection, find as many people as you can to ask for feedback. I would recommend a minimum of five people, and if possible, from different areas of your life: parents, siblings, coworkers, friends, significant others, professors... An easy way to pick people is to think about the different roles you hold in your life and who can evaluate you in each of those.

You will ask your interviewees two simple questions:

1. What are three things I do well?
2. What are three things I could do better?

I like to limit my ask to only three things for each question, because it forces the person to give you the three *best* things you do well and the three *most critical* things that you can improve. When you leave it open to giving as much feedback as they want, they end up giving you very basic things and thinking those will be enough. When you create a cap, you are asking them to prioritize what is most important.

Here are a few tips that can help you have a successful feedback session:

- Arrange a meeting or call with the people from whom you want to get feedback. Don't just email or text them; find ways to do this exercise face-to-face (in person or online through some kind of web-conferencing platform). Making a personal connection helps the other person to be more open, and it gives you the opportunity to make them feel comfortable as well.
- Send the questions you have in advance and ask your interviewees to be prepared. Give them some time to think about their answers before the meeting so they can come with the best feedback possible.
- Make sure they know you won't take anything personally and that your main goal is to learn more about yourself. Some people have a hard time telling others what they could do better because they think they might hurt their feelings. Tell them that you are ready and eager to take whatever they want to tell you.
- Your job at the meeting will be to **listen and take notes** (use your journal!). You will only listen, you will not fight with anything they have to say. You are allowed to ask for examples of when they think you did something or acted a certain way, but if the person can't think of any, don't worry or press them. Just take notes about everything they say. Your responsibility in this interaction is to make them feel comfortable throughout the whole process.

Data analysis

When you get done with your data collection, you will need to analyze it in order to find personal points of improvement. Here is the step-by-step process of what to do:

1. Categorize the data: After taking notes from all the meetings, compile the feedback in a more concise way by looking for themes in the answers of each question. Look at what people said about the things you do well and the things or that you could do better to find common points and group them together. People told me I was good at impacting people, understanding people, and being empathetic. Even though I knew those things were different from one another, I group them into the overall theme of "understanding people." Find a way to count the frequency of certain things people tell you as well, so you know what the bigger themes are in each category.

2. Analyze the data: After looking at the more general themes, write down what you learned about yourself from the feedback. What are the main "takeaways" from what was said? What are the good things they told you that can serve as a boost? What are the things you can improve? Were there any surprises? What got your attention? Summarize your thoughts into one or two paragraphs.

Implementation

This is the final phase of your research—the part where you take the main lessons from your feedback and transform them into action. Write down what you are going to do about what you learned. Create a minimum of five actions that you can start implementing to create positive change. For me, an action I took was deciding to step back each time I felt challenged by someone, and come back to the conversation after reflecting on it. Besides that, I took action to begin thinking about next steps for my career. For you, think about some of the things you can start doing to get closer to the best version of yourself.

Recognize that the changes you want to see will not happen in the matter of a single day. This is all a process and it takes time, but the initial step you took to become aware of what things need to change in your life is one of the hardest and most important steps. Now, it's up to you to be more conscious and apply the feedback to your life little by little.

<u>Extra - Group Exercise: The Honey and Roast</u>

When I was writing about the feedback process, I remembered one of my favorite events while working with the Leadership Development Program. It was called "Honey and Roast." Once a semester, the students would get together for a group feedback session. Basically, we would sit in a circle and choose one person to be praised (the honey) for two minutes and then given two minutes of improvement-based feedback (the roast). One by one, every four minutes (two for honey and two for roast), we went around the circle giving feedback to each other.

I love this group activity because it's an invitation to practice feedback, which means that everybody who comes is ready to give and receive it in the best way. They all come to the event knowing the goal of the activity -- to help each other be better. I gained great insight during this activity, learning that I should slow down and enjoy some "Di time," something the students invented to tell me to stop working so much and take more personal breaks. I also learned so much about my students, which created a deeper connection through the vulnerable moment we took part in together.

Takeaways

- With feedback, I wanted to do two things: reaffirm what I knew about myself with the hopes that it would boost my courage, and look for things that I could improve upon as a person, leader, and educator for others.

- Sometimes, who you really are may not be the same as who other people think you are. The actions that show our true selves are often not aligned with how we want other people to see us. Feedback is a great way to balance this, and to make sure that our actions are being seen by other people in the way we want them to be seen.

- Think about what the best version of yourself looks like (to you), and then think about how your actions, decisions, and behaviors are helping you to reach that person. The best version of yourself doesn't only define where you are now, but also where you want to go. And always remember, it's your decision, not anyone else's.

- Think of feedback as a kind of research that you are conducting to improve yourself. In a simplistic way, we need to collect data when doing research, analyze it, make conclusions, and implement the findings.

- The most crucial aspect to remember is that the feedback you give or receive needs to be used in order for it to have been beneficial. Think about this for a second: feed(it)back. Any input you collect should be at least considered and reflected on before dismissing or implementing.

- Your job when receiving feedback is to listen and take notes.

CHAPTER 05

How To Get Good At Making Decisions

Every time you say you can't do something, it's because you haven't yet made a decision.

I was listening to a podcast once, and I really won't remember what it was called here, but the person on it was talking about why people have such a hard time changing their lives. One of the hosts said, "Every time you tell yourself, 'I can't do this,' change it to 'I don't want to do this.'" That quote simply blew my mind. Basically, every time we can't change what is happening in our lives, it's because we haven't made the decision to do so yet. At that time in my life, I was at a point where that was exactly my excuse.

After I came back to the U.S., our organization was facing some challenges in Brazil. I was the only person on our team who was able to travel full-time around Brazil doing speeches and workshops. Everybody else had a primary job and was putting extra hours into making Movimento Journey happen, so it was hard for them to ask for time off to travel and do our work. When I came to the U.S. and was no longer around to do the traveling, we had to restructure our company and figure out what our next strategy would be. After we spent some time trying different things without much success, I caught myself saying, "I don't know why we can't make this happen; nothing is working." After listening to the podcast and learning about decision-making, I realized the reason why nothing was working was because I hadn't made the decision to make anything work.

I gathered the team together and told them about the big realization I had. I told them that I personally hadn't made the decision to make our company work in a different way, and that maybe we as a company hadn't made that decision either. After discussing it for a while, we decided to try more ideas and make the company work the best way we could. We created a new strategy, launched a series of online workshops to make up for the inability to travel in-person, and made significant progress.

I was very proud of everything we were doing for the company, but over time we started to slow down again. We had a second discussion as a team and decided that maybe Movimento Journey wasn't meant to be. I had personally given all I could, and I knew everyone else had as well. We knew how much we had done in our three years together and we were satisfied with the success we had after training almost four thousand people. It does hurt to say that we had to let it go, but I say it with pride because of the day we made a decision to try everything we could. Because of our team-work, we were able to go our separate ways professionally after Journey concluded, and we stay in contact to this day. We left with our heads held high. I'm eternally grateful for the people who believed in my crazy dreams and fought alongside me throughout that journey. Through Movimento Journey, I grew as a person and as a leader, and I know that our team had to go through that experience to be able to put a period on our story together and begin our individually incredible stories.

The main point here is that everything started with a conscious decision about how we were going to live our lives from one point forward. Without a conscious decision, our brains make automatic decisions for us to lessen our cognitive load. The problem with this is that it will not guarantee you getting where you want to be or where you deserve to be. In fact, our brain makes 35,000 decisions a day... How many of those do you think you are making consciously?

We might think we are making conscious decisions about our lives, but in reality, our brain is automatically deciding things for us. Our brains have a built-in system to make decisions, so to save energy, they end up making a bunch of them without our conscious thought. The problem with this is that, depending on how well your decision-making system has been configured, your brain might not be great at making those automatic decisions for you.

If you are someone who is always negative or has a hard time seeing the good in things, it may be because your decision-making system has been configured like that. If you are a person who is positive about life, it's because your brain was configured like that. How? You did that for yourself. The conscious decisions you make about your life set the configurations and patterns your brain will use to decide automatic and unconscious decisions.

The best way to break from a cycle of negative thoughts is by starting to make conscious and positive decisions about the experiences you have in your life. When you start being more conscious about the decisions you are making, you create better connections in your brain that, in the future, will help you make better unconscious decisions. For example, let's say that you always get nervous in front of audiences. That entire feeling could change with a simple decision to practice ahead of time for your next presentation and decide nothing more than to learn from the outcome. If you can create better experiences for your brain, you will be educating it to make unconscious decisions differently in the future.

What happened in your past has definitely had some kind of impact on you, but it does not determine who you are going to be in the future. It is what you decide to do about your past that makes you that person. We can reconfigure our brains by making more conscious decisions to create the lives we want. Many people believe that things happen for a reason, and maybe they do. At the same time, I also believe that we give reasons to why things happen. Humans have an amazing power to create reasons for everything. If we know how to use that power effectively, we can give meaningful and powerful reasons as to why things happen and increase the quality of and happiness in our lives as a consequence.

Think about it
What are the things you've been telling yourself you "can't" do? Experiment by changing the I "can't" to the I "don't want to." How do you feel about it? Are you ready to make that your decision?

How to get good at making decisions

This might be the simplest answer in the whole book. The best way to get better at making decisions is by simply making more of them. It's about practicing decision-making anywhere you can. The more decisions you make, the more you will feel like you have control over your life. Additionally, you will feel more confident about making decisions and improve your unconscious decision-making.

Understand that we are not only talking about big decisions here, but any decision you might make throughout a typical day. Personally, I was never very good at making small decisions, like what to order from the menu or what gifts I should buy for people. The way I got better at this skill was by forcing myself to make decisions when put in situations like this and try not to overthink the results. Every time I go into a restaurant, I start my experience by making one simple decision: Am I going to order the same thing as always or am I feeling like something different? After deciding that, I face the consequences of my choice -- whatever they may be. Sometimes I get surprised by a new dish, and often I'll either learn that I like a food or that I dislike a food. Overall, the most important aspect is that now I feel less pain in making small decisions because, little by little, I got better at it and understood that something like a bad dish is just part of the process.

If learning how to ride a bicycle requires you to accept the fact that you are going to fall down a few times, learning how to make good decisions requires you to accept the fact that you will make bad decisions on occasion. When riding a bike, if you fall once and decide not to try anymore, you will never learn how to ride successfully. Falling is a part of the process. When learning how to make good decisions for yourself, if you make a bad decision once and decide never to try that again, you will never get good at that skill. Making bad decisions, failing, and making mistakes are all part of the process.

Since we are talking about falling, I remember when I began learning how to skateboard. The first thing I learned how to do was fall. Believe it or not, there are many different ways you can do that, but there is also a way to do it safely. This is a lesson I learned in an experimental judo class as well. They teach you to fall first so that when you do, you don't hurt yourself as badly as you could. What I want to teach you first about making decisions is how to make bad ones. If you know the steps you can take after making a bad decision, the impact of one will not be as bad as it could be.

Overcoming the fear of making bad decisions is a decision in and of itself. What makes us who we are is not what happens to us, but the decisions we make about what happens to us. A bad decision is only a bad decision if you think it is. You may have heard before that failure is only failure if you don't learn anything from it; failure is the event, learning from the failure is the decision. Therefore, we are who we are because of what we decide for ourselves. You are not your past and you are not your future; you are what you decide to be. The more conscious decisions we can make about our lives, the better our decision-making system works when we need it to do so automatically.

Sometimes, all you have to do is prove to yourself that you can do something once, creating a memory that says "I have done it before, so I can do it again."

Types of decisions you can make

If you want to start practicing how to make decisions, here are a few decisions you can start making right now. Tony Robbins recommends that people start making decisions in three different areas: what to focus on, what things mean to them, and what they are going to do about what happens to them. I used this concept here and complemented it with some other ideas from other authors as well as myself.

You decide what to focus on

Attention was always something that companies fought for. The difference is that a while ago, they were doing this through TV and billboard space; today, everything circulates on the Internet -- social media, email marketing, ads everywhere. It almost seems like corporations know better than you do what you need to see or buy.

Advertising is everywhere, and it gets overwhelming. There is too much information on which to focus, and depending on what your social media is made up of, what you see will either leave you feeling good or bad. It's no surprise that reading bad news makes you feel bad and reading good news makes you feel good (maybe even hopeful or happy). The way you feel is related to what you pay attention to, but what most people don't realize is that how they allocate their focus is a choice.

I conducted an experiment once where I didn't go on social media for a month. I was feeling very anxious and couldn't figure out why, so I decided to step away from everything and begin some self-discovery work to try and find the answer. I reduced my phone's screen time from 31 hours a week to 14 hours by cutting out social media, and because of that I felt much more relieved and happy, simply because I was turning my attention toward other activities I enjoyed like reading more, watching TV shows, and even playing some video games.

Beyond that, every time I got back onto social media, I felt even worse than what I had been feeling previously. Realizing this made me think about how I had probably become used to feeling bad, since bad news was all I was seeing. Escaping the reality of social media allows you to acknowledge that the culture it creates is not normal or healthy. Therefore, when I started to go back onto social media again, I deleted some content I didn't want to see anymore. I got pickier about what got my attention, and as a result I had more time to myself and began to feel better over the course of my day.

The negative effects of social media should come as no surprise, but it takes actually depriving yourself of it to realize how much it changes your whole being. In his book, *Happiness by Design: Finding Pleasure and Purpose in Everyday Life*, Paul Dolan says that our happiness is totally related to the way we allocate our attention.

Have you ever heard the saying "What you focus on expands"? If you focus on the bad things, they take up your mental space. If you focus on the good… you are happier. If you think that you are not as happy as you could be, it's because you are allocating your attention to the wrong place(s).

Energy works the same way

If you have ever played video games, you know that most characters have a life bar, right? Usually, when the game starts, the bar has 100% of its life (or energy), and depending on how the game goes, the bar gets reduced little by little. It turns out that we also have life bars. You wake up every morning with a bar of energy filled to 100%, and you get to spend that however you like throughout the day. Every decision you make about where to give your energy is responsible for taking a little or a lot from your overall energy bar.

Based on that concept, making smart decisions about how to spend your energy will be crucial to creating a sustainable way to spend your day. In other words, if you are smart about the way you allocate your attention, you will have more energy throughout your day. If you focus your attention in the right places, you will be focusing your energy into making things happen better and faster for yourself.

In the book, *Essentialism: The Disciplined Pursuit of Less,* Greg McKeown talks about the importance of how much you can grow if you learn how to focus on the essentials. His process is based on exploring, eliminating, and executing. It's when we explore and subtract things from our lives that we can add quality to what we do. Therefore, knowing what is important to us and where to focus our attention helps us to do things with more quality, time, and fulfillment.

If you go through life spending your limited energy everywhere, you won't be able to grow at the rate you want. A lot of people are living like that right now, without a focus and without a direction. They are simply getting things done. However, when you walk for miles without looking where you are going, you might (and probably will) end up in the wrong place. Getting things done is important, but getting things done toward the direction you want to go is even more critical.

This is why, any chance I get, I reinforce the importance of taking a break and reflecting about the direction your life is headed. I encourage you to make a hard stop every Sunday or the first day of every month to evaluate your direction and be sure you are spending your energy in the right places.

> **Think about it**
> Have you been stretching yourself too thin? In other words, where have you been spending your energy lately and how do you feel about it? If you had the chance to stop doing one thing, what would it be? How would you spend your energy better?

You decide what things mean to you

We talked before about the importance of giving the proper meaning to the "best version of yourself," and of getting feedback from others. We went over how the way you define your best self is related to the way you feel about it. That's something you can decide about basically everything in your life, by the way. Define success for example; think about what it means to you. What does it look like? How do you see success?

The way you define something like success totally changes your perception of it. If you tell me that you need to make a million dollars a year, have a big house, and own your dream car to be successful, great! But if you tell me that waking up and getting out of bed every day is your way of being successful, that's great too. For a second, I want you to think about which one of those two are easier to reach. The second one, right? It's easier to feel successful just by waking up than by achieving the money, home, and car goals in the first example. The way we define things is related to the way we feel about them. If you can give it a meaning that is reachable, you are much better off.

Now, let's take the word "friendship." How would you define friendship? What needs to happen so you feel like you have a friendship with someone? For me, friendship is about support. I must confess that I'm not the best at keeping in touch with my friends, but that doesn't mean that I don't care about them. I'm always thinking about them, wishing for their success, and, once in a while, sending a message to see how they are doing. I'm not the kind of person that needs to talk to my friends every day or week to feel like they love me. I don't need personal contact all the time. I also make sure that my friends know that, because if we have different definitions for friendship, problems will inevitably arise. The way you define things not only influences the way you feel, but also how other people feel about you.

From the previous two examples, we can see how giving the proper meaning to things can influence the way we feel about them and about our relationationships. There is another way that you can use meaning in your life, and it might be the most important one we will discuss: the meaning we give to our experiences. We will explore this in more detail in chapter seven. Giving a strong meaning to a bad experience will transform it into a powerful memory that can be used in the future by our brains. What makes us who we are is not what happens to us, but the meanings we give those things.

You decide what you are going to do about it

Very often we blame the world for the things that happen to us. As it turns out, you can also make the choice to blame yourself for the things that happen to you. You can't do anything about how the world reacts, but you can do something about how you are going to react to any given situation.

Locus of control was first seen around the 1950s and was developed by psychologist Julian Rotter. The theory is related to the way people see the events in their lives. When something goes wrong, do you have a tendency to blame others or yourself? Let's say your sales team is not performing the way you want, or maybe your soccer team lost, or maybe you can't get a job. Who is at fault for those things?

There are two locus of control: internal and external. People who have an external locus of control tend to blame external factors for the circumstances of their lives. If their sales team is not performing well, it's because the employees are bad at their jobs. If their soccer team lost, it's because the defense didn't work hard enough to stop the other team from scoring. If they can't get a job, it's because the market is too crowded. People who have an external locus of control always blame everyone and everything... but themselves.

People who have an internal locus of control tend to blame internal factors for the events that happen to them. If their sales team didn't perform well, it's because they didn't train the employees well enough. If their soccer team lost, it's because they missed shooting opportunities. If they can't get a job, it's because they aren't looking for it in the right places or they need to do something to become more attractable to companies.

The important thing to understand from these contrasting views is that you don't have control over the external factors in your life. You can't control the people you work with, you can't control how your teammates are playing, and you can't control the executives at the companies where you are interviewing. Oppositely, you do have control over what you do when each one of these situations occurs. Great leaders attribute the victory to their teams when everything is going right, but when things go wrong, they also find a way to take the fault.

I always noticed that people talk about politics on social media and give their opinions on which candidate is right or wrong. One day I asked myself, if those people could spend the same amount of time doing something to help people as they do complaining and arguing, we would have a much better world. People spend so much time talking about everything that upsets them and blaming other people or the world for their problems. They try to be right and prove their views to friends and family, but in reality, none of that will change much, will it? The same people doing all of this complaining, unfortunately, are choosing to not be directly in control of any situation. Instead, they could go and volunteer their time somewhere, proving their points through actions and assigning agency to themselves.

When you complain about something but don't align your actions with the view you are sharing, it's the same thing as saying that we should save the environment and then passing by trash on the ground rather than picking it up. Change only happens when you take ownership of your world. If you are not happy about something, do something to create change. Fernando Anitelli is a singer and songwriter who says, "Do not accommodate what bothers you."

When leading your own life, you can blame whomever you want for your mistakes or lack of success, but that won't change anything. It's only when you take the responsibility for the things that happen to you that you are able to grow. So, next time you catch yourself blaming others for something that happens, stop and reflect on how you can do something about it to create a better life for yourself. There is always something you can do.

Exercise - Reflecting on your decision making

To conclude this chapter, we will reflect on how you've been making decisions and the things you can do better. Get out your journal and think about the following:

1) Where have you been focusing your attention and energy? What are the things that have been sucking up your energy? Where do you wish to spend more energy and attention? What are some of the changes you can start making right now?

2) Are there recent events which have been bothering you to which you can give a better and stronger meaning? Are there things you perceive as "bad for you" that you can change, translating the meaning to something powerful that will push you forward instead of pull you back?

3) What is something you've been blaming on the world or others that you can take ownership of in this moment? What can you do about it?

Takeaways

"Every time you tell yourself, 'I can't do this,' change it to 'I don't want to do this.'" Basically, every time we can't change what is happening in our lives, it's because we haven't made the decision to do so yet.

What happened in your past has definitely had some kind of impact on you, but it does not determine who you are going to be in the future. It is what you decide to do about your past that makes you that person.

- The best way to get better at making decisions is by simply making more of them. It's about practicing decision-making anywhere you can. The more decisions you make, the more you will feel like you have control over your life. Additionally, you will feel more confident about making decisions and improve your unconscious decision-making.

- If learning how to ride a bicycle requires you to accept the fact that you are going to fall down a few times, learning how to make good decisions requires you to accept the fact that you will make bad decisions on occasion.

- Sometimes, all you have to do is prove to yourself that you can do something once, creating a memory that says "I have done it before, so I can do it again."

- If you think that you are not as happy as you could be, it's because you are allocating your attention to the wrong place(s).

- Knowing what is important to us and where to focus our attention helps us to do things with more quality, time, and fulfillment.

When leading your own life, you can blame whomever you want for your mistakes or lack of success, but that won't change anything. It's only when you take the responsibility for the things that happen to you that you are able to grow.

CHAPTER 06

How Habits Work

We are made of habits

Our whole lives are made up of habits. We have our morning routines, our sleeping habits, our eating habits, exercise habits; everybody has their own weird thing. I love waking up, making coffee, reading for about 30 minutes, and taking a shower before really starting my day. It's almost like if I don't do these things, the day won't be as good as it could be. My body got used to this routine, and every time I get out of it I feel like something is wrong or missing.

The same way we have good habits, we also have bad ones. For example, I have a sweet tooth that is hard to control. After every meal, my body craves something sweet. Chocolate is my favorite, and a big jar of Nutella doesn't last much more than a week with me. At one point in my life I even kept a jar by my bed so that a spoonful of Nutella could be accessed by me 24/7. Since we are on the topic, for other chocolate lovers like me, please check out the recipe for a Brazilian dessert called a brigadeiro. It's super easy to make and will be well worth your time!

If we can learn how our habits work, we will better know what we need to do to create or change them. The path we take to work, the patterns we use to brush our teeth, the way we talk, the way we listen, and the way we see life are all habits we have that keep us going from the time we wake up until the time we go to bed. The more we can understand our own habits on a deeper level, the more we can get to know ourselves and who we want to be.

Think about it

Later in the chapter I will guide you through a step-by-step for how to change or create new habits, but it would be useful if you start thinking now of some habits that you want to change or create. This way, you can start imagining how the examples below fit your case.

The habit cycle

One of the books that changed perceptions about habits is the classic, *The Power of Habit,* by Charles Duhigg. Charles says that a habit is formed through three phases: the cue, the routine, and the reward. The cue is what will kick off the habit. It's the trigger that will initiate it. The routine is the "habit" per say, it can be a mental, physical, or emotional response to the cue. Finally, the reward is the prize your brain gets for indulging in the habit. It's the immediate pleasure you get for completing the routine.

Every habit has a need behind it. People who smoke have a need to feel relaxed or powerful while holding the cigarette or cigar. People who workout have a need to be healthy or are very conscious about their appearance. Being clear about the need (or the why) for a habit helps to increase the emotional intensity of the habit and the chances you have of sticking with it. There is a difference between wanting to create the habit of eating healthy because you "feel like it" and making healthy eating a habit because you want to live a longer life with your wife and kids.

It's also important to understand that our brains are muscles that are constantly changing. Neuroplasticity is the brain's ability to reorganize itself based on the needs of an individual by creating new neural connections. Basically, every time you do something for the first time, your brain creates a new neural connection. When you repeat that action, habit, or behavior, you reinforce that neural connection and make it stronger. That's why, to create a habit or get into a routine, repetition is key. Experts say that it requires about 30 days of consistent practice for new habits to form.

How to create new habits

A lot of people want to develop a reading habit, so I'm going to use it as an example here. Before even trying to do it, people say reading is boring and that it is hard for them to stay in one place while staring at a piece of paper. If you are not clear about the why behind wanting to start this habit, it will be hard to do! When I started my own business, I was clear on needing to set an example for others and being an expert in my subject area so people would respect me. This was my "why" behind beginning a reading habit. I didn't have enough money to participate in trainings, so the main way I had access to information from big names was through reading their books.

After figuring out my clear "why," I had to start thinking about the first phase of habit formation, the cue. An important tip for this is to find something that is pleasurable. I decided I would read in the mornings while drinking my coffee, since morning is one of my favorite times of the day. I thought to myself that maybe introducing something new during that time would make my brain find pleasure in reading. Therefore, my cue was breakfast and my morning routine.

The next step was to create the routine, which in this case was actually reading. With this, it is important to either set a realistic goal for the day or do the activity (reading) until you feel like it's been pleasurable. I say that because what people often do is make the mistake of forcing themselves to read 50 pages or for a whole hour when they are first beginning on their habit creation journey. If your brain has a bad experience with that from the start, it won't want you to repeat that habit. Start small and build your habit up in intensity over time.

For me, there are two kinds of rewards: one is emotional and the other is tangible. Because I know myself well enough, I know how important progress is to me. As an emotional reward, everytime I read I count the pages and write the total down in my journal. Besides that, I always wanted a big library. The only way I could put a book on my library shelf was if I finished it . My shelf wasn't only the place I put my books, but the books on the shelf represented "awards" for being a reader.

After a while of practicing this habit, I realized some interesting things. First, since coffee was part of my cue, I realized that If I wanted to read at any time, having a cup of coffee nearby always gave me some kind of motivational boost. Additionally, after the behavior became a habit, I started to enjoy reading at any time of the day. Today, I love reading when I'm traveling and sometimes before bed as well. The cool thing about creating a habit is that it eventually gets to a point where it becomes part of who you are.

How to change a habit

Now that you understand how to create a habit and know the basics of the process, let's see how we can use the same concepts to change a habit. As an example, we will use the most infamous and evil habit of the new age -- the smartphone. We know how addictive phones can be and how the time we spend online stacks up every day without us even realizing it.

The first step is to identify the process. What is the cue, the habit, and the reward? When you think about smartphone use in the most simplistic way, the cue would be every new notification you get or every time you feel bored. The actual habit would be picking up the phone and checking your social media, email, or other apps. Finally, the reward might be the sensation of being loved by the people liking your pictures, the progression of your life by going through your timeline, or the pleasure of clearing your notifications.

After identifying the components of the habit, we can try to act on the different parts of it. We start by acting on the cue, making it harder to trigger the habit. In the case of smartphones, a way to make it harder to be bothered by the cue would be to put your phone in another room, deactivate the notifications, or even hide the most used apps. In this way, we are making it harder to act on the trigger.

You can also act on the habit to change it. In our example, there are apps that track the time you spend on social media so that you realize how it adds up. There are also apps that limit the time you can spend scrolling on your timeline. Another solution is to substitute the habit you want to change with something different that will bring you the same reward. Using a different example, I realized once that I was drinking too much coffee. I thought I needed it to get work done and keep me awake, but I found out I could get the same effects (rewards) by drinking decaf tea. My need wasn't to have the coffee in particular, but to have *something* to drink while I work.

Always remember that to change a habit you need to be clear about the "why." The only way to break a habit is by creating a different one to take its place. When you stop looking at your notifications or limit your time on social media, you are not only getting rid of the habit of spending hours on your phone, but creating the habit of being more conscious about your time online. The key to changing your habits is to try different things and see how they work for you. Sometimes your creation or replacement strategies will work, other times, they won't. As long as you have a good "why" and enough repetition, you can change or create a habit for yourself.

Why we procrastinate

While in many ways, habits are unique to the person who possesses them, there are many habits that are common among people that we must work to avoid. Procrastination is one of these common habits. In his amazing TED talk called, "Inside the Mind of a Master Procrastinator," Tim Urban does a fun and interesting job explaining how our minds work.

Tim uses the example of when we need to get a big project done in three months. We typically tend to split the workload into equal parts and plan to do a little bit every day, right? Before we know it, the first month is over and we haven't done a thing. It's okay though, because there are two more months to finish. We replan everything and get ready to finish the work in just two months. Well, then the second month ends and still nothing gets done. We replan once again to get it all done in a month. Soon, there are three weeks left, then two, then one… and the last day before the deadline is when most of the work gets done. This is the general path we take when we have a lot of work to do; why do we indulge in this kind of behavior?

Tim says that inside our minds we have something called the "Rational Decision Maker" and this is responsible for making all the conscious decisions about our days. This is the thing that decides to get work done, for example. We also have an "Instant Gratification Monkey," which is what is responsible for any instantaneous pleasure we might crave, like looking on our phones or eating chocolate while on a new diet. When you first receive your project, the Rational Decision Maker decides to get work done, but the Instant Gratification Monkey is the one that spends the next three months procrastinating. It's the one that decides to do the dishes, eat, binge watch *Friends* for the 500th time, and spend hours and hours on social media.

That happens until the "Panic Monster" shows up. The Panic Monster is the only thing the Instant Gratification Monkey is afraid of, so when the monkey sees the monster, he runs away. The Rational Decision Maker is able to take control of your mind again. The Panic Monster, represents your deadline, or any kind of pressure or bad consequence that might come from not getting your work done. Every time we have a deadline, the Rational Decision Maker takes control of our minds to get things done.

We haven't brought the conversation back to dreams in a while, but here we go. A problem we face when thinking about dreams is that most of them don't have a deadline. This means the Rational Decision Maker might never gain control of your mind to make your dreams come true.

Basically, we procrastinate achieving our dreams because we believe that in the moment, it's more painful to do something to get closer to them than to stay on the same path. When you are in front of your computer and you decide to look at your social media instead of getting work done, it's because the pleasure of using social media is higher than the pain of not getting work done. When the deadline gets closer, the pain of not getting work done becomes higher than the pleasure of procrastinating. Finally, you decide to do something about that pain. Many times, people simply don't take initial action and instead put off responsibility because they link too much pain to the act of getting things done, and too little pain to the fact that they could be missing an opportunity.

Think about it
What are some of the things you have been procrastinating a lot lately? Has the panic monster showed up yet?

Using pain and pleasure to change your habits

This pain and pleasure concept is something I first saw in the Tony Robbins book, *Awaken the Giant Within*. Tony makes it clear that every move we make in life is to either avoid pain or to gain pleasure. He says, "If we link massive pain to any behavior or emotional pattern, we will avoid indulging in it at all costs."

Understanding this is extremely important when you need to compensate for the Panic Monster that might never show up. Remember, we only encounter the Panic Monster when we have a hard deadline or when something scary will happen if we do not follow through on our responsibilities. Other times, like with dreams, we need to create an ally to help us when there is no pressing due date. We can use the concept of pain and pleasure to create habits and change our behavior to get us closer to where we want to be. If we can link enough emotion to the pain or pleasure of the habit or action we want to take, the chances that our behaviors will change are very high.

Most people make decisions about what will create plea-sure or pain in their lives based on the short-term rather than thinking about the long-term. Let me give you an example: I have always loved exercising. As it turns out, there comes a point in your life when you get very busy and late nights working mean the only things you can think of are going home, taking a shower, and doing something fun (or going to bed). At the same time, as you get older, the habit of exercise becomes more important for your overall health and wellness. When I was lacking in motivation, I decided to use this con-cept to re-motivate me into action.

If I started to think about the long-term pain of not exer-cising, the first thing that came to mind was my future family. I don't have kids yet, but creating a family is a huge dream I have. Not exercising today reduces the number of days I'll get to play with them. I plan to have kids when I'm around 35 years old; that means that I'll be 55 when they are 20. I want to have the energy to play with them and do fun things when they are young. If I'm not healthy, I won't be able to do those things, and I even run the risk of something happening with my health before they are even born. So my future kids are a huge motivation of mine today.

People use this same concept to stop bad habits like smoking or eating poorly. It's up to you to figure out what may cause a lot of pain or pleasure in your life. Playing with pain and pleasure might be incredibly motivating, but remember that anything valuable you desire always requires some short-term pain to achieve the long-term result. If you can understand the long-term pleasure you are looking for, the short-term pain will be easily supported.

Think about it

How can you apply the concept of pain and pleasure to create a panic monster even in the absence of a hard deadline? What is it going to cost you if you don't achieve your dreams? What is the pleasure you will gain if they come true?

Extra tips to create or change habits

So far, we've seen how habits work and discussed the importance of emotional charge and repetition in the process of creating or changing habits. We also saw how pain and pleasure can be of assistance to us on our journeys. Here are some more things that help us to create new habits in our lives:

Keep track of your progress

Earlier in the chapter, I explained how I used to track the pages I read to keep progress and serve as motivation to keep going. Recording your goals is important because it gives you a sense of how you're doing (remember how we talked about feedback being so important?). Progress is addicting, and when you track your progress, you can see the areas that could use improvement.

Recently, the COVID-19 pandemic has caused many parks and gyms to be closed. This has made exercising some-what difficult at times. The options left for me to exercise were to work out at home or run outside. I never liked to run, so I tried (not very hard) to exercise at home and it didn't work very well. I decided then to invest in the outside runs. Again, I'm not a fan. At the same time, I know I am a progress-seeker, so I thought maybe keeping track of my runs would help me feel more motivated to get them done.

The first time I ran, I aimed to be out for 20 minutes with no expectations of pace or distance. I wrote my results down at the end and my goal was to then improve on something every run. I could go 100 more feet, one more minute, or make some kind of improvement on my speed. Then, every five runs I would calculate the average progress made. Overall, I wanted to see better time, distance or pace using my averages. I kept this habit for about 45 days. When gyms reopened in my region, I'm proud to say that I started to enjoy running and was able to run five miles in 55 minutes, which was a victory for someone who almost passed out after initially running two miles nonstop.

It's very important to find a goal-tracking method that works for you. My brother was on the same running challenge as me, and he decided to track his progress in an Excel worksheet. I got my data from the Apple app and input it in my journal. There is something for everybody and you might have to try different strategies before finding the right one!

Have milestones

There is no point in tracking your progress if you don't have milestones you are looking to celebrate. Sometimes it is hard to see the final product of a habit and because of that it can be hard to set a goal. Milestones are like stepping blocks that get you from the starting point to achieving your long-term goals. My running was improving every run, and I looked forward to calculating the averages every five runs. For my reading, I always had a goal per week of pages I wanted to read. With writing I followed the same process ; I had a goal for words written over a certain period of day.

Think about the milestones you can set for your new habit(s) and remember that the last item of the cycle is the reward. Don't forget to celebrate yourself when you achieve your milestones. I'm not asking you to throw a party every time you do something good, but rather to find special ways to celebrate both small and big moments. I love celebrating my progress with some pizza or a good cup of Brazilian coffee. Think about what gives you pleasure and use it to celebrate your success.

Activation energy

In chemistry, the term "activation energy" is used to describe the minimum energy needed to activate a chemical reaction. When a reaction happens fast, it means that it has a low level of activation energy. When the reaction is slow, it's because it has a high level of activation energy. We can apply this concept to habits as well. We want to decrease the activation energy needed for good habits and increase the activation energy needed for bad habits.

If you want to start the good habit of reading, a way to decrease the activation energy would be by putting a book by your bed. If you want to run in the mornings, maybe you could sleep with the clothes you will run in so you don't have to get ready before leaving your house.

In the case of changing bad habits, if you want to eat healthier, don't buy chocolate or unhealthy foods so you won't have easy access to them in your house. For my earlier Nutella example, I hid the jar in the back of my highest kitchen cabinet so it would be hard for me to see when I went looking for a snack.

Tell other people about it

One of the first non-fiction books I ever read was *The Psychology of Persuasion* by Robert Cialdini. Robert is an expert about persuasion and talks about six core principles that can help us to influence people. One of my favorites is the consistency principle; Robert says that people have the desire to be consistent with what they have already said or done in the past. For example, have you ever committed to doing something with a friend or family member, regretted committing, and done the thing anyway because you said you would? That's the consistency principle in action.

This is an excellent strategy we can use to create a new habit. Humans have an inner desire that pushes us to form consistency between our actions and our words. We can use this principle to force us to commit to new habits as well. A simple strategy might be just to tell your friends that you are reading more. This might make you feel more inclined to actually start reading more (because you don't want to have to go back on your word). The coolest thing about this principle is that when you are consistent and you model the way for yourself, you are "trustworthy" and people see you as an example.

Get an accountability buddy

Having someone to hold you accountable means having someone who dismisses your excuses. This is a very effective technique to reach your goals. To do this, you can do something as easy as asking a friend to join the road to your goal with you. You can ask your friend to workout with you or to take turns cooking something healthy for dinner. You can join (or create) a book club with a friend if you want to read more. Think about who you can count on in your new journey and get them involved.

Use sticky notes

It never hurts to leave reminders for yourself to get things done! In the beginning, it can be hard to remember the details of your new habits, so having sticky notes around to remind yourself of what you need to do is a good strategy. I've seen people leave small notes on their fridge that say, "Don't even think about it," discouraging them from unnecessary snacking, or notes on top of books that say, "Pick me, please!" Think about how you can remind and motivate yourself to execute your new habits.

Everything takes practice

Anything in life takes practice. Any behavior you have acquired throughout your life took practice, even the behaviors you want to change. A nice point of reflection is this: What kind of bad behaviors, bad thoughts, or bad emotions have you felt or acted out lately? Isn't it crazy to realize that you only felt that way or did that thing because somehow you created that habit? Unconsciously, you created the habit of feeling, thinking, or acting the way you do.

I was talking to a friend once about bad habits humans have, like the need to compare ourselves with others or the fear of rejection. He was telling me about his love life, and how after more than a year after his last breakup he wouldn't talk to another girl because he was super afraid of rejection. As it turns out, by not trying anything he was reinforcing the habit he had toward fearing rejection. He was protecting that identity. Additionally, our brains don't know what is real and what is our imagination. Because of that, all the times my friend was imagining himself being rejected by anyone he liked also reinforced the habit of not wanting to be rejected. The worst part is that he was doing this to himself unconsciously; he had no idea about this pattern. The same thing goes for our comparison habit. By looking into social media and checking up on what our friends are doing constantly, we are reinforcing the tendency to compare our lives to theirs.

What I'm inviting you to do now is consciously create a new habit and a new way of living your life. As I said, it will take practice! I'm not sure where I heard this, but **every day you don't create a habit is another day that you create the habit of inaction**. Every day you don't create the habit of exercising is another day that you create the habit of not exercising.

Every day you don't create the habit of eating healthy is another day that you are creating the habit of not eating healthy. I'm inviting you to change your mindset and your behaviors. If you do that consistently, change will happen for you. Every day you don't is another day that you are delaying the control of your life and the opportunity to make good decisions.

Exercise - The habit challenge

Let's try to put all of this into practice. I gave you a few questions to guide you through this new journey of changing or creating new habits.

1. Write down a habit you want to change or create, or an action that you've been putting off and want to get done.
2. Write down why you want to change this habit or get this action done. What is the future pleasure associated with taking responsibility here?
3. Write down what it will cost you if you don't change now. Remember, the uglier, the better!
4. How can you decrease or increase the activation energy for your new habit (the cue)?
5. How can you track the progress of your habit? What are some milestones you can create?
6. How will you remind yourself about the habit? Can you use an accountability buddy?
7. How will you celebrate the milestones of your progress?

Takeaways

It's also important to understand that our brains are muscles that are constantly changing. Basically, every time you do something for the first time, your brain creates a new neural connection. When you repeat that action, habit, or behavior, you reinforce that neural connection and make it stronger.

Basically, we procrastinate achieving our dreams because we believe that in the moment, it's more painful to do something to get closer to them than to stay on the same path.

Many times, people simply don't take initial action and instead put off responsibility because they link too much pain to the act of getting things done, and too little pain to the fact that they could be missing an opportunity.

Playing with pain and pleasure might be incredibly motivating, but remember that anything valuable you desire always requires some short term pain to achieve the long term result. If you can understand what is the long term pleasure you are looking for, the short term pain will be easily supported.

What I'm inviting you to do now is consciously create a new habit and a new way of living your life. As I said, it will take practice! Everyday you don't create a habit is another day that you create the habit of inaction.

CHAPTER 07

How To Learn From Experiences

The day I got lost in the woods

I want to share with you one of the most stressful experiences I've ever had. I call it *The Day I Got Lost in the Woods.* It's also an article I published on my social media platforms, so maybe you've read it before.

> I thought that it would be another Sunday morning, very chill and relaxing.
>
> I was wrong.
>
> My girlfriend and I woke up, had a nice breakfast, and then decided to go for a hike. Good weather on the weekends had become rare since we were approaching winter. But that Sunday was so beautiful, super sunny with a blue and clean sky and a temperature around 60 degrees. It was a perfect day to be outside and enjoy nature. Off we went to Bell Smith Springs, a national natural landmark located in the Shawnee National Forest in Southern Illinois.

Once there, we were amazed by how beautiful the place was. The water was crystal clear and the rocks and trees combined with the fall style made the morning breathtaking. In a couple hours, we had seen many of the places around our initial location. Since it was early, we decided to try the longer trail.

Why not, right?

It was a 3.2-mile hike that should have taken around two hours in a spectacular place. After an hour on the trail, everything was great. We were following the blue markers on the trees, watching our steps, and looking out for any dangerous animals. It was perfect. I fell on my back in one of the waterfalls and she tripped on one of the rocks when we were crossing the river, dipping her feet in the water. These were fun events that we laughed about.

We kept walking and laughing about everything. It was a great morning. We walked a little bit more and took some pictures. We walked a little more and crossed the river. We walked a little bit more. And more. We kept walking until we realized that we hadn't seen a blue marker on the trail for a while. We kept walking to see if we could find one. Nothing. We decided to walk backwards and find the last blue mark. Nothing. Little by little, we realized that we were lost.

We were lost.

It is still hard to express the feeling of being in the middle of nowhere and not knowing at all where to go. Every time I tell this story to someone, I still don't feel like they understand how scared I was for us. Many things crossed our minds while we were walking and trying to find a way out over the next two hours. Eventually, we climbed a high hill and found service to locate where we were. We were miles in the opposite direction of where we should've been. Right there we had to make a decision between going back to the initial point or walking towards a road that was a mile and a half in the opposite direction. We decided to try to find the road, because we might not have had enough daylight to walk back through the woods. After a while using a compass, we finally found the road. We celebrated a lot, but the journey wasn't yet complete. We still had to hitchhike back to where our car was.

At the end of the day, we were safe and thankful for everything we had.

On the way back home, we reflected on everything that had happened and how it happened over the course of the day. We thought about all the lessons we could take from our experience and brainstormed what we would've done differently if we had to go through it again. These are the lessons we came up with:

Keep walking

It's easy to freak out when you are lost. When we realized that we were lost we started to think about the worst things: What if we don't make it? What if it gets cold? What if we run out of food? What if we need to spend the night here? We both had many of those destructive thoughts, but we didn't communicate them to each other. We kept a positive attitude, encouraging and checking on each other all the time. We kept walking.

Life is the same way. Many times we are lost and we don't know what to do, but we have to keep walking. We need to have and feel progress. It is all too easy to jump to the looming negative thoughts, and if you do, they will bring you down. If you just keep walking, focusing on what's next instead of the problem at hand, your body and brain will find a way to help you. We need to keep a positive attitude and check on each other while we all keep moving forward.

When you have a goal in mind, you do whatever you have to do

It was funny that in the minute we figured out where we needed to go, we gained back our energy and motivation. Walking through the dense forest, getting cuts on our legs from the branches, tripping on big logs… everything felt irrelevant compared to our big goal of finding that road—and surviving.

Life is the same way. In the moment that you find your big goal or dream, you become unstoppable. You are willing to face whatever challenges life throws at you because you want to achieve that one end goal so badly.

Stop and re-evaluate

After we climbed that hill and figured out where we were, it was too risky to keep using our phones since the batteries were low. We decided to use the compass on one phone instead, and let it guide us to the road. Eventually, we were able to check our location on her phone to make sure that we were still heading in the right direction. We made a stop just about every five minutes to see where we were and re-evaluate our route.

Life is the same way. Sometimes we need to stop and rethink where we are at or adjust our route. When you know your dream, it's always good to stop and evaluate where you are every once in a while. This way, you can see where there is room for improvement and analyze how to get closer to where you want to be. If you don't know where you want to go yet, stop and re-evaluate then also. Maybe you need to try a different route!

Be around the right people

My girlfriend and I joked at the end of our journey that we didn't know if we would've made it the way we did if we were around other people. We were very positive and encouraging toward each other and we never let negativity get us. Beyond that, when we had to hitchhike, we had to be careful about from whom we would take a ride. Thankfully, those who offered to drive us—Carolyn and Clyde—were the best we could've asked for.

Guess what? Life is the same way. You have to be around the right people and make sure that they encourage and support you along your journey (and that you do the same for them!). Don't be afraid to ask for extra help, but also be careful about who you ask.

Always have a knife, a lighter, and a flashlight

One of the things that we will do differently next time we go hiking will be to bring a knife, a lighter, and a flashlight. Our mistake was thinking that, because we thought it would be an easy trail, we would not need too many supplies. Even though we wouldn't have needed to use these resources at all, having them would've made us feel more secure in the event that we had to spend the night in the woods.

I guess the lesson here is that it's never bad to be over-prepared for life. The problem when we are under-prepared is that we always regret it later and think extensively about how clueless we were for not putting the extra effort into preparing ourselves for the unknown. Always be a little extra and do a little bit more to be as ready as you can be for unexpected challenges. That way, you won't need to overthink if (or when) something goes wrong.

It was great.

Overall, getting lost in the woods was a great experience. It's what we call type two fun: It's hard in the moment of the experience but you laugh afterward. Maybe that's life in general, right? We often overestimate the impact of the bad experiences we have, when in reality they are just more experiences that we get to laugh about and learn from in the end.

You are what you live

I love this story because it was one of the worst experiences in my life. How ironic? Luckily nothing bad happened, but the overall experience gave me a lot to think about. I also love that we were able to look at what happened with learning eyes, trying to figure out what we could've done better or could improve on for next time. We could've just as easily said that we would never go hiking again. Instead, we learned and went on more hikes together (better prepared, of course).

A key piece of information I learned about myself through this experience was that I was able to keep myself calm during a stressful situation. The awesome thing is that now I use this experience as a base for other stressful situations in my life. "I've been lost in the woods before and I am ok. This will be easy!"

Experiences shape who we are. When you think about the things you believe, your strengths, and your weaknesses, many times they come from an experience you had in the past. If you are a persistent person, maybe that's because you've been through a lot and have been rewarded by never giving up. If you are a believer in your dreams, maybe that's because your parents always incentivized you to believe in yourself and supported your crazy thoughts.

Paulo Vieira, a Brazilian coach and writer, talks about the 90/10 rule. Any person who drives a car faces the risk of a car crash. Understand that the car crash is 10% of the event. A whole 90% of the event is what you are going to do about it in the event that it occurs. When the event happens there isn't much you can do about it, but you can control how you are going to react in the aftermath. You can storm out of the car and blame the other person or you can hurry to make sure that other person is okay. You don't always have control of what happens to you, but you can control what you are going to do about the things that do happen.

Finding meaning in our experiences and questioning what our realities look like is crucial. Think about situations you've been in with your friends where you all have the same physical experience (an adventure like mine or maybe a class you took together). Did you all enjoy it in the same way? I bet you didn't. I'm betting you all had different interpretations of the experience and took different lessons from it as well.

Netflix has a very interesting docuseries called "The Mind Explained." In one of the first episodes, experts talk about memory and how our brain fills in the blanks for all aspects of experiences that we cannot remember. Studies show that we actually only remember about 50% of a total experience; everything else is our brains completing the story using our imagination.

This is pretty wild when you think about all of us humans living in the same exact world. We all have different interpretations of identical experiences. Many people go through the same things in life, but some people struggle while others persevere. Why is that? I believe it is partially because of our ability to give meaning to the experiences we encounter. The way you describe an experience and the meaning you give to it is 100% correlated to how you feel about it and how it stays in your memory.

Getting lost in the woods, for example, can be something that will make you never want to go hiking again or something that will make you eager for your next trip. Think about experiences you have had in the past and how they have helped shape you into who you are. If you had given a different meaning to your experiences, do you think the person you are today would be any different?

If I had given a bad meaning to getting lost in the woods, I would never want to be in a similar situation again and would avoid it at all costs. My life would be shaped differently than it is now because of that. However, because I gave that experience a strong meaning instead, I'm more willing to put myself in situations that are similar again. I also use the experience as an internal motivator to do things that scare me. This pushes me torward trying new things rather than being fearful of new experiences.

The key to life in this respect is to be more mindful about what we go through, how we talk about our experiences, and the meanings we give to them. Who you are is not what happens in your life, but rather what you do about what happens in your life.

DIOGO SEIXAS

A note about experiences

If experiences shape who we are, there is nothing more important than accruing more experiences to grow and learn more about ourselves. One thing I have learned is that the decision-making process gets more complex as you get older, and where you have been matters for where you go next. My personal theory is that when you grow, you acquire more responsibilities: a relationship, family, bills, etc., and because of that, when you need to make a decision you have to weigh more items on the scale before choosing the best path.

If you are young, you have the gift of detachment. Use that as much as you can to make mistakes and learn from them! Don't be afraid to go out into the world and try different things. Personally, one of the commitments I made to myself was that I would not worry about stability until my 30s because I wanted to give myself as many opportunities for new experiences as possible. I sought out mistakes and failure, but also an incredible and enjoyable life.

The only way to learn something new is by experiencing it. When someone tells me they are lost in life and don't know what to do, my first thought is to ask them to do experiments. What you do outside the classroom is as important (if not more important) than what you do inside it. If you don't know whether you want to become a teacher, an engineer, or a ballerina, try them all. You have time. You can volunteer for a local group to teach people something you are passionate about. You can go to a local factory or an engineering company in your city and ask for a tour or to talk with some of the employees to explore the job. You can learn ballet and perform in a local theater. Try new things and learn as much as you can about yourself from them.

If you are older and have more at stake in terms of making big decisions, or are afraid of big changes, take small leaps of faith. For example, if you are thinking about making a career change, before quitting everything and jumping into a new job, you can experiment in smaller ways. Maybe you can volunteer somewhere in the area you want to move to, maybe you can talk to someone in the field you are looking to switch to about their experiences. Maybe you can start creating your business, but instead of going full-time right away you can implement one or two smaller ideas to get your feet wet. Be creative and find ways to create life experiments; there is always a way to experience what you want on a smaller scale. This is what I call forming "prototype experiences."

Think about it

What are the experiences that have shaped you? If you had to choose just one, what would it be? Why was it important? What did you learn from it?

Prototype experiences

A prototype is nothing more than a trial. When you have a future planned and you know all of the possibilities, you can start taking small steps towards the future. The mistake many people make is focusing on the final goal, such as being a successful business owner, for example. However, there are other things that need to come together before becoming successful (including mistakes and failures).

In the startup world today, there is always talk about "failing fast." The key to failing fast is to also fail small. For example, you want to open a Brazilian restaurant in a U.S. city. Before raising any money, building a facility, hiring people, or selling your goodies, you might start by cooking a few dishes and inviting your friends over to try them. The next step might be trying to get some outside orders so you can cook from home and deliver to your customers. If that works out, you might hire another person to help you, open a take-home facility, and *then* move toward opening a full restaurant.

Ask yourself: What is the smallest and easiest step you can take to move toward what you want? Remember that you are first creating a trial of your plan before making any huge changes. Thinking about what needs to be tested before continuing with a big idea is extremely important.

The reason we start small is to make sure we are not moving toward something we might not like or enjoy. How can you say you want to be a professor if you have never tried to teach before? How can you say that you want to run your own company if you have never tried to lead a group of people before? How can you say you want to become a novelist if you have never tried writing a short article or story before?

Life is all about experimenting. We can only figure out what we truly want if we try it out and learn from what happens. I love saying that I learned everything that I didn't want to do with my life in college. The classes I took were great to understand how things worked, but also to select the things I didn't want in my life. To me, college was an important experience but is also a full-time experiment.

Experiments bring about experiences, and those shape who we become. I know this concept might initially sound scary, but it gets better when you understand the power of giving meaning to what happens to you. Like everything else in life, it takes practice and the process gets easier every time.

> **Think about it**
> What is an experience you've been afraid of giving your-self? How can you prototype that experience so that if you fail, you do it safely?

What is the difference between a positive and a negative experience?

The difference between a positive and a negative experience is in the meaning you give to it. If you fail in a class and tell yourself that you suck as a person and a student, your overall experience might be labeled as "bad." If you go through the same experience but tell yourself that you had to fail in order to learn that things aren't always easy, it becomes a positive experience.

It's also important to learn the difference between *being positive* and *giving a positive meaning* to what happens in your life. A positive person always thinks that things will go right, no matter what. Life is a rainbow and it will be perfect all the time. This is a great way of thinking about life as long as you are ready to deal with the hardships when they arrive, because they will; I know, you know.

Jim Collins, famous author of the incredible books *Great by Choice, Built to Last,* and *Good to Great,* talks about "The Stockdale Paradox," where "you must maintain unwavering faith that you can and will prevail in the end, regardless of the difficulties, and at the same time have the discipline to confront the most brutal facts of your current reality, whatever they might be."

Collins wants us to win, but he also wants us to know that it's important to acknowledge that things might go wrong, so we need to be strong and face the consequences when they do. He wrote this concept with the differences between companies that last and companies that don't in mind, but we can apply it to our lives as well. We need to have faith that things will work out but we also need to have the tools to deal with our realities when they don't. That's when knowing the power of meaning makes such a difference.

If we can find meaning in everything, no matter what, the chances are that we will always learn from it and improve our lives.

You are going to fail anyway

Since we have been talking about the importance of meaning for a while now, let's practice it one more time by defining what failure means to us. How would you define failure? What does it mean to you? How do you see it? Remember again that the way we define things is directly related to the way we feel about them. In other words, if you define failure as something bad that makes you look unintelligent, that's how you are going to feel. Defining failure as part of the process of life where you grow and improve makes you more willing to risk and fail.

The reason why we need to talk about failure at length is because you are going to fail no matter what. You are going to fail as a student, an entrepreneur, a wife/husband, a parent, and a person. I'm sorry, but the hard truth is that failure is inevitable. Actually, you've been failing forever. Am I wrong?

Therefore, learning how to deal with failure is an important part of life.

I can't count how many mistakes I have made. I can't tell how many times I did something "wrong." It was only because I was willing to fail that I made progress in life. When I first started Journey in Brazil, we were just three 23-year-old boys wanting to make some change. We failed as a team, but we learned from it. I failed as a speaker, but I learned from it. I failed people, and that hurts a lot. In the beginning of my journey as the LDP Coordinator, I remember a couple of scenarios where I wasn't listening to my students as well as I could have. In one instance, I had a student who was struggling with self-confidence and I gave them the help *I thought* they needed. I thought my job was done and that the student would figure it out on their own eventually. Well, that didn't happen, and the student ended up leaving the program. It wasn't only my fault, but I knew that I could've done a better job as a coach to help them with their struggles.

Do I feel bad because those things happened? Of course I do! At the same time, I'm extremely grateful for the experiences because they helped me to become the person I am today. By working as the LDP Coordinator and encountering these students, I learned that behind the outward demonstration of one problem, there is always something deeper. Now, I tell myself that it's up to me to notice that. Today, before holding someone accountable for something, I check up on their life to see if there is anything else that might be holding them back.

Everything you do and every experience you have helps you to become the person you want to be. It's up to you to reflect on them and to give the proper meaning to each one. You will make thousands of mistakes over the course of making your dreams come true, but it's because of them that you learn how to get what you have always wanted.

We are all just trying to survive

Why are we so afraid of failing? It's connected to our survival instincts. Basically, the human being was trained to be more negative than positive. When our caveman friends were trying to survive many years ago, they had to look for any sign of danger around them before they could set up camp. Therefore, everytime they were in a new place, they had to look for any possible predators or threats before they could feel safe.

The world may have changed, but we never lost our survival instincts. Every time we are doing something new or going through a new experience, we still look for that feeling of safety. To feel safe, we have to eliminate the threats; because of that, we end up looking at the negatives of a situation before we look for the positives.

This goes beyond just setting up camp. In the book *The Happiness Trap: Stop Struggling, Start Living*, Russ Harris talks about other behaviors we have kept from the days of caveman friends. He points out that today, it's not a saber-toothed tiger or wooly mammoth that our mind warns us about. Intead, it's the idea of losing our jobs, being rejected, embarrassing ourselves in public, getting cancer, and so on.

For cavemen, it was important to belong to a group and fit in to increase the chances of survival. Today we continue to look for that inclusion aspect; we want to be accepted somewhere. Thousands of years ago, whoever had the best tools would survive. Today, we measure who is "surviving" by who has the bigger house, best car, or highest-paying job.

Harris concludes by saying, "thus, evolution has shaped our brains so that we are hardwired to suffer psychologically: to compare, evaluate, and criticize ourselves, to focus on what we're lacking, to rapidly become dissatisfied with what we have, and to imagine all sorts of frightening scenarios, most of which will never happen."

But, as always, there is hope. We need to train our brains to be okay with what is "bad." If we don't teach our minds to look at the good things around us, a pattern of negativity might take control of our lives and the outcome won't be the best. To look toward a better life, we need to develop something called "failure immunity."

Failure immunity

"Failure immunity" is a concept created by Bill Burnett and Dave Evans that I first saw in their book *Designing Your Life*. It means failing so many times that you get used to it. When this happens, failure becomes part of your routine and your life. As a consequence, you take more risks because you know any outcome won't hurt you *that bad*.

I only became comfortable speaking in front of people because I was willing to take the risk of being in front of people. I did it so many times that I ended up developing a set of beliefs and techniques that allow me to be comfortable in those situations today. I've been through so much as a speaker that whatever happens from now on happens, and it won't affect me too much.

The coolest thing about failure immunity is that once you develop it for a certain area of your life, that ability gets transferred to other areas as well. Because I got used to making mistakes as a speaker, I was more willing to make mistakes as an entrepreneur. When I got used to making mistakes, I decided to challenge myself by doing some podcasts, then videos, and now a book. All of these things were once things I was once super afraid to do, but because I developed some failure immunity from past experiences, I'm more willing to try things that scare me. I've done hard things before and I'm still here, so what is the worst that can happen?

Honestly, the biggest thing I fear is living a life of regrets. For me, the pain of having regrets is higher than the pleasure of my comfort zone (remember when we talked about the pain vs. pleasure concept?). I would rather do something that makes me feel challenged than cling to my safe identity. There is only one way for me to know if I will succeed or not, and that's by trying.

One of my favorite TED talks is by Larry Smith, a professor of economics at the University of Waterloo in Canada. He talks about why we will fail to have a great career. Larry gives honest feedback to the world, in a very funny and grumpy way, on why we will fail in life. We make excuses like "I'm not lucky," "I'm not good enough or smart enough;" we blame things we cannot control or other people for our problems and we feel sorry for ourselves. Smith asks us to imagine a world where we tell our children: "Go for it kid, just like I did." We don't want to be parents who tell our kids to pursue their passions; you want to be an example to them to follow their dreams.

Larry finished the talk saying that the most hurtful words you can say to yourself start with, "if only I had…" These words focus on regret. Although some things might be hard and scary, at the end of our lives we won't regret the things we did, but the things we didn't do when we wanted to do them. If we are going to fail no matter what, why not fail in something that matters?

How to reframe failure

Now, you might be wondering how you can develop some failure immunity of your own. The important point to remember is that fear will disappear when you act on it. Therefore, as much as you try, the better you will get. At the same time, this process will be easier for you if you can change the overall perspective you have about failure. Here are some things you should look to reframe or understand so you can be more comfortable about failing:

Give failure a strong meaning: Rethink the question I've given you before about what failure means to you. Give it a strong meaning that makes you want to fail, so that you can grow. Tell people about it, post it on social media, give people advice. Remember, the way you talk about your past can change your future.

Stop comparing yourself to other people: Everybody is different. Everybody has a different life, different goals, different struggles, different fears, and different motivations. Stop comparing who suffered the most, and who got there faster, who got further, and stop questioning the ways in which someone achieved. Just respect people for getting to where they are. If you don't want to be compared with anyone else, you have to stop comparing yourself with other people as well. Focus on what you have on your plate and work with that. You probably have heard the saying that "we shouldn't compare their stage with our backstage." Everyone else deserves to be where they are, and so do you.

People don't care: This is probably one of my favorites, but also the one I struggle with the most. People really don't care about you. Do you know why? Because you don't care about them. I am a professional overthinker and often get myself thinking about "that one thing" I did or said that may have been wrong: "Did they understand what I meant?", "Was I rude?", "Should I have acted differently?" It turns out that nobody cares. Think about one mistake your not-so-close friend made in the past seven days. How many times did you think to yourself: "That person is so stupid; I can believe they did that." Probably none! So why do you think others are thinking about you right now? People don't care about what you do, because they are too worried about what they've done to you. Stop thinking about those kinds of things; everybody has their own stuff to worry about. Focus on yours.

We always overestimate how bad something will be: One of my students once told me, "You don't remember your ex-boyfriend/ex-girlfriend's last name from 10 years ago." This is very true. Think about your first breakup. You probably don't remember much about the person. Even though the experience must have been very emotional for you, today it probably doesn't affect you at all. That's the way life goes in general. There might be situations happening right now that we think mark the end of something. Maybe we think we won't ever be the same or we won't ever be "normal" again. When you look back though, I bet there have been times in your life when you reached rock bottom but eventually came back. We always do. I bet that if I were to have asked you five years ago and today how much the worst event from your life affected you, I would have got two totally different answers from you. What was so important to you five years ago may not affect you deeply today. So, failure might look bad right now, but in the long-term, you will be glad you went through the experience. It made you who you are.

Think about it
What is your new definition of failure? How can you start developing failure immunity in your life?

The failure step-by-step guide

I'm a person who loves step-by-step. I get mad when I read something about an outcome and people don't lay out how to get to the result they did. By now, hopefully you have realized that I love giving you not only the "why," but the "how" as well. Next, you will find a step-by-step guide with five thoughts you can use to learn from yourself when you have a bad experience or failure in your life:

1) Reframe failure and remember it's a good thing.
   What does failure mean to you? Remind yourself that you've been through worse and you will survive whatever comes next. Remember all the times you grew from your past experiences. Although it is hard when things do not go your way, you have a choice to focus on what you can learn from rather than what to feel sorry about.

2) How can I describe this experience in a powerful way?
    Pay attention to the way you are going to describe
    your experience in the future. We feel what we say.
    There is a difference between "It was the worst ex-
    perience of my life," and "It was one of my biggest
    learning opportunities."

3) What did I learn from this?
    Always look for powerful questions to ask yourself.
    Your brain answers whatever you ask it. Notice the
    differing tones between "Why am I like this?" and
    "What can I do better next time?" or "What can I
    learn from this?" Always focus on what you can learn
    rather than tearing yourself down. Asking powerful
    questions helps you to create a powerful meaning
    from your experience that will change the way you
    feel about it.

4) What am I going to do differently next time?
    Decide what you are going to do from now on when
    encountering similar situations. Based on what you
    learned from this, what would you do differently next
    time? Make sure to write about this in your journal.

Exercise - The Lifeline

To start exploring your experiences, let's take a look at your
life through a timeline format. This exercise came from a book
called *Business Model You: A One-Page Method For Reinventing
Your Career,* by Alexander Osterwalder, Tim Clark, and Yves
Pigneur. We will explore the significant events you have had

in your life, both good and bad. To do that, we will split this exercise into two parts:

1) Think about ten (or more) events that have occurred throughout your life and draw them onto a timeline. If possible, think about a minimum of five good and five bad events for some balance. Try to think of specific events in your life from different areas: personal, professional, social life, love, academics, spiritual, etc. You can also think about milestones or landmarks associated with strong feelings you have had in your life. Basically, you will be drawing a graph of significance based on your experiences. Next, you will connect your events; a positive event will be a peak on your timeline and a negative event will be a valley.

2) After you pick your most significant events, explore them by asking yourself why they are so important to you. Write down about a sentence per event describing its significance and another two or three sentences that explore what you learned from it or why it contributed to the formation of the person you are today. Did you gain skills or abilities? Did you learn something significant about life that then became a value to you?

Remember you are starting your journey of self-discovery, so take your time when doing these exercises and don't worry about what is "right" or "wrong." The experience is different for everybody. I have had many students where, after giving clear instructions on how to do this exercise, they decided to do something different, but it still ended up being great for them. If you want to wander off and add or take things out of the exercise, feel free to do so! It is just important that at the end, you learn something new about yourself.

Takeaways

- Experiences shape who we are. When you think about the things you believe, your strengths, and your weaknesses, many times they come from an experience you had in the past.

- When the event happens there isn't much you can do about it, but you can control how you are going to react in the aftermath.

- A prototype is nothing more than a trial. When you have a future planned and you know all of the possibilities, you can start taking small steps towards the future.

- We need to train our brains to be okay with what is "bad." If we don't teach our minds to look at the good things around us, a pattern of negativity might take control of our lives and the outcome won't be the best.

- "Failure immunity" means failing so many times that you get used to it. When this happens, failure becomes part of your routine and your life. As a consequence, you take more risks because you know any outcome won't hurt you *that bad*.

CHAPTER 08

How To Challenge Our Beliefs

Our "Internal Library"

Imagine that we have a library inside our minds. Every time we have an experience and the meaning is given, the way we feel is registered in this library. We learned earlier that our brains make over 35,000 decisions a day and that it is impossible to make all those decisions consciously. Therefore, our brains use the internal library as a resource to make automatic decisions. It does this because our bodies do anything they can to save energy. The more references in our library, the less we have to consciously think when we need to make a decision.

In a conscious scenario, here is how things happen in your mind: something happens, bad or good, and you have the choice to give meaning to it. Let's say you had a presentation and it went horrible. In that final moment standing in front of the audience, you have a choice to make. You could choose to tell yourself that you suck and will never do this again, or you could decide to learn more about how to give presentations so you don't have to go through that embarrassment ever again. You had one experience that leads to one choice that you are responsible to make consciously. As we know, depending on what you chose, the experience will shape who you are in the future, which in this case would be determined or fearful.

When you don't make a conscious decision, your brain will make an automatic one for you based on your internal library. When you give a presentation that goes terribly wrong, your brain searches in your library to find evidence to support some kind of decision for what to do about it. If you've been a person who has historically been afraid of things, your brain will probably decide that you should never put yourself in front of a crowd again. On the contrary, if it finds evidence in your library that shows you are persistent and dedicated, it will choose the option where you might learn more about giving presentations before repeating the experience.

Think about this number again for a second. If your brain makes 35,000 decisions a day and most of them are made unconsciously, most of the time your brain is deciding things for you based on experience. When considering a person who doesn't know about the power of meaning, for example, and thinking about how her brain will be making unconscious decisions most of the time, a lot of who she is and the things she believes in are decided without her even knowing it.

If you are anxious or calm, depressed or excited, happy or unhappy, stressed or relaxed, persistent or lazy, those attributes are all based on decisions of meaning you made in your past. Each one of those decisions was logged in your internal experience library, sometimes consciously and sometimes unconsciously. This becomes the basis of your "belief system."

Maybe if you are shy, it's because someone made fun of you and you decided not to expose yourself anymore so that wouldn't happen again. Maybe if you have discipline to go after your goals, it's because of swimming classes you took at some point in your life and finally having the courage to jump off the diving board. The good news is that, even after giving initial meaning to a past experience, we can always re-evaluate and re-assign meaning if we want to look at something in a new way. This is how we can change the way we feel and what we believe about ourselves and the world.

Who you are, both good or bad, is worth exploring, and most importantly we can change who we are. Self-creation starts with the decision of wanting to change and the persistence to do it even though it is hard. We will talk about strategies for how to make this happen shortly, but most importantly, you need to know that you can change by logging more positive experiences in your internal library.

How do we develop beliefs

The internal library is also known as our "belief system," the set of beliefs we have about ourselves or the world. Our **beliefs are formed by experiences from our past, things we repeatedly told ourselves, and things other people repeatedly told us that we decided to accept as truth. Our belief systems are also formed by the things we imagine about who we are.** Depending on the emotional intensity you use when imagining something, your brain might accept it as a true event. This happens because our brains can't differentiate between what is real and what comes from our imagination.

As an example, let's use the presentation scenario again. When you had that bad experience giving a presentation and decided never to do that again, you probably told yourself over and over that you are "not good enough" and that you were "not made for this." Additionally, every time you picture yourself in front of a crowd, you picture yourself failing intensely.

You imagine it so many times that you end up dreaming about it and it becomes your worst nightmare. As a result, you avoid every possibility of giving a presentation and therefore, develop a limiting belief.

This limiting belief gets registered in your internal library and might be accessed in the future as evidence for a new decision of whether to experience something. This is called limiting because it will, ultimately, cause limitations in your abilities, thoughts, and life. A limiting belief of "being a bad presenter" forces you to never develop the skill of public speaking and limits you from the consequences of this valuable ability, like meeting new people or just being able to clearly present your work. A limiting belief is what will hold you from doing another presentation when the opportunity arises, because you will tell yourself "I can't do presentations, I suck at them."

Let's say now that you had the same experience, giving an awful presentation, but you decided that you needed to learn and practice more to get good at it. You tell yourself that you are persistent and that you can do the task if you put enough effort into it. You picture yourself being successful and natural during the presentation and the audience being entertained by you. Your friends see your dedication and admire you for reaching your goal, making sure to let you know that you inspire them. When the first opportunity to do a presentation arrives, you jump on it without hesitating and do a better job than ever before. You created a powerful belief.

This powerful belief also gets registered in your internal library for future reference, but, different from the limiting belief, a powerful belief motivates, encourages, and pushes you to use your abilities to improve your life. When you start giving better presentations, you label yourself as a "good presenter."

Because of this, you feel confident about doing more of them and comfortable in social environments. You meet a lot of new people and get offered many different opportunities. A powerful belief pushes you to have more positive experiences because it reinforces that you are skilled and the consequences are pleasurable.

When you develop a belief, you will look for more ways to prove that belief, good or bad. Limiting beliefs are the ones that hold you back from achieving the life you want. Powerful beliefs are the ones that help you get what you want. The good news about all of this is that it is possible to change your belief system, to fight your limiting beliefs and create more powerful ones.

Think about it

How is your internal library today? Does it have more powerful (positive) or limiting (negative) experiences within it?

Growth mindset

One of the big resources for mindset today is Carol Dweck, author of the famous and best-selling book, *Mindset: The New Psychology of Success*. To start, mindset is nothing more than the settings of our mind (get it?). Carol talks about the two kinds of mentalities that we can have: a growth mindset and a fixed mindset.

People with a fixed mindset believe they have a static intelligence. They have the desire to look smart, and because of that they avoid challenges, get defensive and give up easily, see effort as fruitless, ignore negative feedback, and feel threatened by the success of others. As a consequence, they always think they are good and never achieve their maximum potential.

On the other side, people who have a growth mindset think there is always room for improvement. They can always grow and get better. These people embrace challenges, are persistent, see effort as the way to mastery, learn from feedback, and find inspiration in others. As a consequence, they are consistently working toward their full potential and getting closer all the time.

Be happy with who you are, but don't settle for that person. When we look at life with a fixed mindset, we don't believe it's possible to change. When we jump into life with a growth mindset, always trying to learn from our experience, we can constantly evolve. Have a growth mindset when looking at your life; keep learning and observing who you are. Always look for ways to get rid of the limiting beliefs you hold close, and create new, powerful beliefs that can help you achieve the life you want.

At the end of the day, you have a choice about what to believe. You can always question yourself: "How can I look at this experience or belief with a growth mindset?" And as we've seen, the more you do that, the better you get. Someday, you will reach a point where you don't even have to think about it anymore; a growth mindset will just be who you are.

Think about it

What kind of mindset do you think you have? Do you see yourself as knowing everything you need to know, or you are always looking for ways to improve and learn from others? What can you do better to have even more of a growth mindset?

How to change a limiting belief

First, let's be extremely clear about the difference between a powerful belief and a limiting belief. Ask yourself the following questions:

- Does this belief help me to be the person I want to be?
- Does this belief help me to connect with what I truly value?
- Does this belief help me in the long-term to create the life I want?

If you answered "yes" for any of those, you are thinking of a powerful belief. If you answered "no," you are thinking of a limiting belief.

A limiting belief is usually hidden behind an explanation or justification of our lives' failures or limitations. Think about something you really really want, either short-term or long-term. Now, think about why you haven't achieved it yet. All of the excuses you have might be limiting beliefs that you hold about who you are or about the world works. You can tell yourself that you are not smart enough, or you can say that people are selfish and they don't want to help you. Those are examples of both an internal limiting belief and an external limiting belief. One is related to the way you think about yourself and the other is related to the way you think about others.

The problem with limiting beliefs is that usually they are generalizations that we make in our lives. Because our brain believes in everything we tell it, we create limiting beliefs about ourselves. However, we need to understand that a limiting belief is just an interpretation of an experience and that we can go back to question our beliefs anytime we want.

Tony Robbins explains a belief like a table. Imagine that the belief is the table top and the legs are the references—experiences you had, things you tell yourself, or things that people tell you—that support your belief. The idea is that the more legs (references) your table (belief) has, the more emotionally strong the belief will be, good or bad.

The key to this analogy is to add legs to our powerful beliefs and remove legs from our limiting beliefs. When you think about your powerful beliefs, you need to add experiences and references so you can maintain them. For limiting beliefs, it means challenging the references you already have or prototyping experiences which can create new references to a powerful belief.

Let's go back to our "I'm a bad presenter" limiting belief. The legs that support this reference are the experience you had, what you friends told you, and what you keep telling yourself. To challenge this, you can ask yourself, "How many times did I give a presentation that went poorly?" If it has happened only once, your personal experience is only one reference that is supporting the entire table. Is there any way you can reframe the meaning of your experience to become something more powerful? How many times have people told you that you suck at presenting? Were they coming from a good place or were they only trying to mess with you? Think about what you've been telling yourself, is it true or is it an excuse to not repeat the experience again out of fear?

Then, how can you prototype experiences that will help you create a powerful belief about your ability to give a presentation? What are the experiences you need to have to believe that you are a *dedicated presenter*? Notice that I didn't say "I'm a good presenter," because you are in the *process* of becoming one. You can make safer presentations with family and friends who will give you honest feedback. You can join a public speaking class. You can practice over and over and always be on the lookout to give powerful meanings to the experiences you prototype. The idea here is to break the table of limiting beliefs, and at the same time create one for powerful beliefs.

Exercise - Challenging your beliefs

This is a quick questionnaire that you can use to either better your powerful beliefs or challenge your limiting beliefs.

<u>Powerful beliefs</u>

1. What are three powerful beliefs you have about yourself or the world that you can use to push yourself forward?
2. What are some of the references that support these beliefs? What are the legs from your table?
3. Have you been underutilizing these beliefs? How can you use it better? What kinds of actions have you been putting off that will be supported by your powerful beliefs?

<u>Limiting beliefs</u>

1. What are three limiting beliefs you have about yourself or the world that you want to change?
2. What are the references that sustain your beliefs? What are the legs from your table?
3. How can you challenge the references you have? Are they real?

4. What it's going to cost you in the future if you don't change this belief?
5. What are some of the experiences you can prototype to break your limiting beliefs, and how can those prototypes then serve as references for your new powerful beliefs?
6. What can you start doing right now to create that change?

Takeaways

🔑 Each one of those decisions was logged in your internal experience library, sometimes consciously and sometimes unconsciously. This becomes the basis of your "belief system."

🔑 Our beliefs are formed by experiences from our past, things we repeatedly told ourselves, and things other people repeatedly told us that we decided to accept as truth. Our belief systems are also formed by the things we imagine about who we are.

🔑 When you develop a belief, you will look for more ways to prove that belief, good or bad. Limiting beliefs are the ones that hold you back from achieving the life you want. Powerful beliefs are the ones that help you get what you want.

🔑 People with a fixed mindset believe they have a static intelligence. They have the desire to look smart, and because of that they avoid challenges,

get defensive and give up easily, see effort as fruitless, ignore negative feedback, and feel threatened
by the success of others. On the other side, people
who have a growth mindset think there is always
room for improvement. They can always grow and
get better. These people embrace challenges, are
persistent, see effort as the way to mastery, learn
from feedback, and find inspiration in others.

- A limiting belief is usually hidden behind an explanation or justification of our lives' failures or
  limitations.

- When you think about your powerful beliefs, you
  need to add experiences and references so you can
  maintain them. For limiting beliefs, it means challenging the references you already have or prototyping experiences which can create new references to
  a powerful belief.

CHAPTER 09

How To Be More Motivated

What is motivation?

For me, the best way to define motivation is this: **motives to action**. It's hard to find motivation for things when you don't have a motive behind your actions—a reason for doing. The more you can get to know yourself, your goals, your purpose, your beliefs, and your experiences, the more content you can use for your motives to action. People who know themselves well know how to find motivation; people who don't know themselves at all have a harder time figuring out how to drive themselves to get things done.

Daniel Pink is an expert about motivation and in his book, *Drive*, he talks about how the concept of motivation has evolved over the years. He calls Motivation 1.0 the "survival motivation," the one that covers our basic needs required to stay alive. Motivation 2.0 is based on the Carrot Stick Theory: If you do a task right you get a reward, and if you do it wrong you get punished.

Finally, the "new motivation," Motivation 3.0, is based on three pillars: autonomy, mastery, and purpose. Daniel says, "As humans we have an inner drive to be autonomous, self-determined, and to have a connection with people and the world." Autonomy is the desire we have to control our lives and make our own decisions. It's the sense of choice you have about what to do and how to do it. Mastery is the desire to get better at something that matters to you. It's a never-ending process of getting better. Purpose is the desire to contribute to something that is larger than ourselves. Next, let's look into all three and find how we can use them to be more motivated.

Think about it
What are your motives to action?

Autonomy

Autonomy is one of our biggest motivators. We want to feel like we are in control of our lives and are making conscious decisions about what to do and when to do it, where we want to go, and how we are going to get there. Autonomy is about us, not about what other people tell us. In my view, not many people understand that they have the control over this. Throughout life, we have been untrained to make decisions by ourselves. There was always someone deciding for us: parents, teachers, friends, etc. That's why when we get lost today, we have a hard time deciding things to get us back on track. Lucky for us, we can regain our autonomy by continuing to expose ourselves to decision-making opportunities.

As we saw before, success, failure, and even happiness are all based on decisions we make for ourselves. I believe that if you got this book, you want to be in control of your life and you want to do what nobody else is doing. That's a great start! If you haven't realized this yet, this book is pretty much all about autonomy. So far, we've learned about how our experiences, habits, feedback, and journaling can affect our decision-making. We continue by covering purpose, goals, direction, and happiness. I'm not telling you what you should do, but I'm giving you the tools to make your own choices. The decision to use them or not is yours, but I can say that when you decide to take control of your life and change what you think is not working, it's liberating.

And addicting. When you understand the power of autonomy and you use it, you don't want to let it go. Today, I'm very conscious about what I do and why I do it. I'm trying to be as conscious as possible when planning my next steps and understanding the way I feel about things and talk to/about people. I feel like I am in control, although life plays some tricks sometimes. However, I feel motivated and empowered to keep doing the best I can.

To feel more motivated and gain control over your life, you can start by making more decisions. An excellent way to do this is by doing the exercises in this book. That's why in this chapter I won't give you any more specifics about autonomy, because the whole book is about making decisions to change your life and journey for the better.

Purpose

I guess purpose is one of the things with which everybody struggles. As Dan Pink discusses in his book, purpose is the desire to contribute to something bigger than ourselves. The way I see it, purpose gives us a sense of direction and gives us what we *need* instead of what we *want*. Purpose is the reason behind everything; it is your "why" for what you do. Think of purpose as something you feel good about when you are doing it. It is something that gives you a sense of fulfillment, a sense of doing something that matters. It is something that makes you feel complete, both when you are doing it and when you are done. It makes you get lost in time. It's something that just makes sense for you.

Many people get overwhelmed by the fact that they don't feel they have a purpose when everyone tells them they should. First, don't worry about not having a purpose. In my personal opinion, you don't need to have a set purpose. You should just always be looking for it. Where? I don't know. Prototype experiences, try new things, take adventures, but keep looking no matter what. Finding your purpose is a lifelong journey. Some find it earlier than others; some find it later and that's okay, too.

For most of us, our purpose will also change over the years. When I was in high school and about to go to college, my only purpose was in joining a big company and becoming an executive so I could have a chill life with my family. When I joined AIESEC I became passionate about helping people, but I wasn't sure how to do it. After joining the Leadership Development Program, I fell in love with leadership, and because I had a good time giving presentations for AIESEC, I thought that maybe I could teach leadership and help people. I had a few experiences doing that with different age groups and the population that I liked the most was college students. So, I decided I wanted to teach leadership for college students as a way to help them better their lives. During this decision-making process, I learned more and more about self-improvement and became very interested in helping younger generations lead their own lives. This book is one way I am trying to do this. Purpose grows over the years and changes as well. I bet that mine will keep changing as I get older and experience new opportunities. That's why it is important to be conscious and reflect on all you have done. We learn a lot from ourselves, and we don't even really know that until it happens.

Purpose is a crazy thing; sometimes we live by it and sometimes we have no knowledge of it at all. Sometimes a purpose can be big and sometimes it can be small. Some people have a purpose of changing the educational system, curing cancer, or solving world hunger. It's also okay if your purpose is not like that. Maybe your purpose is to eat healthy and be an example for others. Maybe it is to promote the power of reading books, or even helping people consume less information from books and instead from more digital products. A purpose doesn't have to be something radical that will change the entire world for everyone, but it is your contribution to changing the world you are in. Purpose can be related to the environment, it can be related to your job, or to any specific role you play in your life. Doctors are health guardians. Teachers are future builders. Look at your life and understand the contributions and impacts you have made and can continue to make.

You can find purpose in what you do for your job or in your community. It's all about the way you see things, and guess what? It's also about the meaning you give to the things you do. There is a famous story of a time when President JFK visited NASA and found a man cleaning the floor. JFK introduced himself and asked the man what he did at NASA. The man said "I'm helping put a man on the moon."

Right now, ask yourself what you are doing for work and what the "why" is behind it. The purpose and the "why" are very similar. The famous author Simon Sinek talks about the importance of knowing the "why" before the "how" or the "what." Communicating the "why" to others or to ourselves connects with our "feeling brain." Since we are guided by emotions, we *feel* more inclined to do things when we have a reason. The "why" is what makes us get out of bed every morning; it's what makes our hearts beat and what makes us feel like we are doing something good. Two very good books about this "why" are *Start with Why,* by Simon Sinek and *Find Your Why: A Practical Guide for Discovering Purpose for You and Your Team,* by David Mead, Peter Docker, and Simon Sinek.

A final word of advice on purpose is to not only think about what your purpose is, but also what your purpose is not. If you are doing something that it's not as fulfilling as you thought it would be, try something else. We talked about prototyping experiences and trying new things on a small scale earlier. That's a great way to find your purpose. Remember, it's a lifelong journey, and you can find purpose anywhere. That will never change.

Exercise - Finding purpose

I would highly recommend you take a look at Simon Sinek's work. He has a TED talk called "How great leaders inspire action" that explains the basics of his theory. Besides that, take a look at Mark Manson's article "7 Strange Questions That Help You To Find Your Life Purpose." This is a fun piece that gives you a different perspective on purpose. I also identified a couple exercises below that might help you as well.

Questions to explore purpose

1) Think about experiences you have had in your past that were meaningful to you. What made you feel good about them? What made you feel like you lost your sense of time? What made you proud? If you want, you can go back to your timeline exercise for this.

2) If you didn't have to worry about money, how would you spend a full year learning new things? This isn't necessarily asking about formal education; it can be anything you'd like. You can go as far as you want with this.

3) If you had one million dollars to spend right now, what would you do with it? What would you buy? Where would you live? With whom would you live? (Please, choose something else other than traveling as your main source of spending.)

Purpose statement

I adapted this exercise form the book *Business Model You* by Alexander Osterwalder, Tim Clark, and Yves Pigneur. This activity helps you think about purpose from different angles to create your overall purpose statement. I like this exercise because it challenges your imagination to combine activities you like to do, people you would like to help, and the ways in which you would like to help those people.

We will go through a few steps, and at the end you will combine all the steps to form the first draft of your purpose statement.

Step 01: Think about things you like to do in general. What are the things that make you forget about time? What are the things you really enjoy doing? You can also think about times when you had a meaningful experience (that one time volunteering, or that one internship you had). You can take a look at your answer for question one from the previous exercise. Describe these experiences in a few words. (For example: A meaningful experience I've had was that one time I did a presentation about a project of which I was a part.)

Step 02: If you had to summarize your activities or experiences from above with just one verb, what would it be? Think about how you can use your experiences to help someone. Give one or two action verbs per experience listed in step one. (For example: to present, to talk, to inform, to educate.)

Step 03: What kind of people were involved in your meaningful experiences? What kind of people could benefit from your experiences? Most importantly, what kind of people would you most enjoy working with? (For example: companies or students.)

Step 04: Now we will put everything together. Connect all three steps, starting with the action verb, then the people you want to help, and finally, the activity through which you will be helping them. (For example: I want to inform and educate students through presentations and training.)

I understand that it might be a little confusing at first, so make modifications as you see fit. I would also encourage you to create three or four different statements and combine them all at the end. Depending on how it goes, you might create something very interesting!

Remember that finding your purpose will go beyond an exercise on a piece of paper. Although this might challenge your imagination, your true search is in the experiences you have gained. If you say that you would like to teach people, find a way to volunteer and test your theory. As a consequence, you will know if you'd like to keep pursuing it or if you can cross it off your list and jump to the next adventure.

Mastery

Finally, mastery is the desire to grow and improve in life. As humans, we have this natural desire to grow in every area of life: personal, professional, health, finances, career, or relationship. We want to feel like we are improving and making progress.

A great way to feel like you are making progress is by asking for feedback (good thing that you already know how to do that). In the habits chapter, we also talked about how tracking progress is extremely important and I told you my personal strategy for that. Progress generates progress and that makes you feel more motivated. Let's look at the actual definition of progress:

Forward or onward movement toward a destination.

Therefore, to feel like we are progressing toward something, we need to know where we are headed. Defining the points where you can grow is very important in recognizing your forward movement. As I said before, progress is addicting. If we can start seeing it in our lives, we won't want to stop acting. That's why it's very important to set goals; they are the destination.

To be clear, when I talk about goals, I'm not only thinking of huge, life-altering aspirations. I'm also thinking about the little things, really any kind of goal or destination you want to reach in the next day, month, year, or decade. To accelerate the process of achieving our goals, we need to find ways of feeling progress; that's why doing something like breaking them down is so important. It doesn't only make a goal easier to think about and attain, it gives us a sense of accomplishment that will motivate us. If you want to run 10 kilometers, first set and accomplish smaller goals, like running one, three, five, and seven kilometers. If you want to open your own business, set smaller goals along the way, like creating your Instagram page or website. Focus on the small steps, not the final objective.

When going for your goals, it is critical to track them. Peter Drucker, a management expert known world wide, said: "If you can't measure it, you can't improve it." When you keep track of things it's easier to know what went right and what went wrong, therefore allowing you to identify room for improvement. The evaluation of your goals is a sub-step that is equally as important to reaching the finish line, and also helps you to feel like you are progressing along the way.

The most important thing after all is said and done is to celebrate. Celebration is an excellent way to praise progress. Acknowledge your improvement every step of the way, that will keep you motivated too! It's not only about the mountaintop, but also about each smaller peak you reach on the way there.

Setting goals, breaking them down, tracking them, evaluating them, and celebrating accomplishments are key components to the success formula for progress and growth. This formula is the key to mastery and to feeling like you are improving in life.

What is balance and when do we need it?

I've heard so many people talk about the importance of having balance in life. One day, my two good friends and coworkers and I were discussing whether it truly is essential. Do we really need balance in life? Thinking about life like an essentialist, if you are spending your energy in different areas all of the time to achieve balance, as a consequence it will be hard to grow significantly in any one area.

So, I ask again: Do we need balance? My personal opinion is that it depends. If you want to grow in a certain area right now, you will have to dedicate enough attention and energy into that area to be able to do so. Because of this, you will lose focus in other areas, which means altering the overall balance of the system. In the long-term, however, at some point in your life, you will feel the need to pay attention to different areas in order to be fulfilled. That's when the balance makes a comeback. If you spend a good part of your life thinking about your career, there is a chance that at some point, you will want to invest time to find a good partner. If you spend a good part of your life looking for a partner, when you find the one, you might focus on improving your career to give yourself and your partner the best lives possible. It's all a matter of choice and *there is no right or wrong*. What is most important to you right now drives your focus and energy toward the areas in which you want to grow.

Sometimes we need to be out of balance to make progress, but (because there is always a "but") when we are out of balance for too long, we have an inner force that wants us to restore our equilibrium.

The key here is always to remember that balance, or lack thereof, is a choice. I like to say that we should always be happy, but never satisfied. There is always something we'd like to (and can) improve. You and I have the choice to focus our attention and energy wherever we want. Occasionally, taking a break from our current focus, looking toward the paths we want to follow, and reevaluating our journeys is a great way to choose what should get our attention next. Let's look into this a bit more now, and aim to set the direction.

> **Think about it**
> Where do you think you have balance right now? Where do you think you need to focus so you can grow and develop more?

Exercise - Setting focus and goals

Brainstorming goals

At the beginning of the book, I proposed an exercise where you think about your big dreams. As a complement to that, I also suggest you complete an "I want to" list, where you think about things you want to have, do, learn, and give. This is a great way to warm up your mind to think about the future. If you haven't done either of those yet, I would suggest making time for that now. If you have already done both, you might use them here as well.

Evaluating past, present and future

In his book *Awaken the Giant Within*, Tony Robbins proposes an exercise to evaluate our past, present, and future. I adapted this exercise a little bit to help us set our focus on what we want to develop and the goals to grow in those different areas.

Let's start by evaluating our past:

1) Start by choosing 8-10 different areas of your life that would like to evaluate. Examples are family, friends, relationships, finances, fun, career, school, health, personal growth, mental health, attractiveness, and spirituality (though there are others!).

2) Evaluate how your life was in each of those areas three years ago. Give this evaluation a score from 1-10 and explain with a short sentence why you scored the way you did for each area.

Now, look at the present:

3) Evaluate the same areas again, but based on how your life is right now. Give them a score from 1-10 and explain your rating with a short sentence.

Reflection point:

4) What did you learn about yourself? Were you surprised? What caught your attention the most? Have you changed a lot over the last three years?

One of the reasons why I like this exercise is because it helps us to break down life into compartments, rather than seeing it all at once. People usually have a vision of their lives as good or bad. Sometimes, because of that one thing that has been bothering us a lot lately, we generalize by saying our entire lives are a mess. When we see life from different angles, though, we realize that maybe one or two areas need attention, but overall, things are good.

This exercise also helps us to understand that everything in life changes, usually pretty quickly. We understand that we have evolved and changed, sometimes in negative ways but for the most part, in positive ways. We learn and grow from our lives all the time without even realizing it; can you even imagine how much of a change could occur if we were consciously focused on growth?

Let's think about the future now:

5) Using the same areas you chose in the first part of this exercise, evaluate how you want them to be three years from now. Give them a score from 1-10, with a sentence describing why you want certain areas to change (or not).

As we saw before, we can't focus on everything at once. We need to choose the areas of our lives we want to focus on the most in order to dedicate the proper amount of attention and energy toward progress.

6) Out of the 8-10 initial areas, choose two or three that you want to focus more on right now. They do not have to be areas you evaluated lower on the rating scales, they can be any you want to work on improving. When looking at what is next in your life, what are the important things you need to focus on? Of course we want to improve all aspects of our lives if we can, but we need to start somewhere.

Now that we have a good idea of what areas we want to focus on, let's get more specific about the changes we want to make in those areas.

7) What are some of the goals you have for the next three years? For a minimum of five minutes per area of life chosen, write down what your goals are for the next three years

8) If you haven't done this yet for each goal you have set for yourself, include a timeline and deadline for when you want to achieve it over the next three years. For example, let's say you decided to focus on your career and you want to have your own company in the next three years. Write the number three next to that goal. If you want to start an MBA program in one year, put the number one next to that goal. Repeat this step for any additional goals you thought of in 7.

The next step is to start thinking about your action plan, so you can get closer to your goals.

9) Choose the goals that are closest to their deadlines and break them down into smaller steps. For example, if the goal that is closest to happening is enrolling in an MBA program, what are the smaller steps that you need to take to get there? Maybe you need to research programs, budget how much you can spend, talk to people who have gone through the programs you like, choose an institution, or get ready for the program's start. Give the smaller steps deadlines too!

    a. Extra: If you want to challenge yourself, you can break down all your other goals into smaller steps so you know what needs to happen first and when. This will give you a broader vision of what you have to do and when it needs to happen.

    b. What are you going to do this week to get closer to reaching your goal? Write down your plan for the week and get things going.

The last step is the best one and involves how you are going to celebrate your goals.

10) Write down how you are going to celebrate your goals, no matter how big or small they are when you reach them. Be clear about what you will do: eat something special, get together with friends, buy something, drink something, take a day off, sleep in the next morning. It doesn't matter what you do, but

make sure to celebrate the small wins. Life is not only about work.

In this exercise, we did very important things:

1) We evaluated life in general by splitting it into different areas;
2) We decided which areas to focus on;
3) We decided what we want to accomplish in those areas;
4) We decided the smaller steps we need to take to reach the big goal;
5) We decided how to celebrate our achievement.

Everything we want to accomplish in life needs to be broken down. If you are clear about the direction you want to go and what you want to accomplish, breaking your goal down is the easiest way to feel progress and practice mastery, which will leave you feeling more motivated.

Takeaways

- The best way to define motivation is this: motives to action. It's hard to find motivation for things when you don't have a motive behind your actions—a reason for doing. The more you can get to know yourself, your goals, your purpose, your beliefs, and your experiences, the more content you can use for your motives to action.

- Autonomy is one of our biggest motivators. We want to feel like we are in control of our lives and are making conscious decisions about what to do and when to do it, where we want to go, and how we are going to get there.

The way I see it, purpose gives us a sense of direction and gives us what we *need* instead of what we *want*. Purpose is the reason behind everything; it is your "why" for what you do.

Mastery is the desire to grow and improve in life. As humans, we have this natural desire to grow in every area of life: personal, professional, health, finances, career, or relationship. We want to feel like we are improving and making progress.

Sometimes we need to be out of balance to make progress, but (because there is always a "but") when we are out of balance for too long, we have an inner force that wants us to restore our equilibrium.

CHAPTER 10

How To Find My Values

Who are you?

I thought it was funny when I saw recently a meme about the LinkedIn Effect. It showed how simple job titles get translated by people on their LinkedIn profiles. For example, a store manager might define herself as a "regional chief leader project manager." A freelancer might define himself as the "CEO of his own one-person business." An HR employee might define himself as a "people potential visionary."

Honestly, I love those titles! I love how people can get creative to show how their employment experiences can translate to something that may be more attractive to employees at other companies. The problem is that people allow themselves to be defined only by what they do. Unfortunately, what they do does not equal who they are.

Think about it, when introducing yourself to people, you usually start with the basics of what you do, right? Here is a personal example:

"My name is Diogo Seixas, and I've been working in leadership and personal development since 2016. I got my bachelor's in Production Engineering, an MBA, and a PhD in Business from

*the Southern Illinois University of Carbondale, Illinois. I'm also
a writer, a professor, and a trainer. Nice to meet you!"*

This doesn't actually tell you who I am though, right? It
informs you what I've done, what I do, and some of the roles
I play in my life.

I learned about this with Murilo Gun, a creativity professor from Brazil whom I introduced earlier. Gun is very
energetic and like me, loves to learn from life. He is always
questioning things that nobody else sees and that somehow we
all accept as "normal." He is one of those people who is constantly asking "What if?" (Which, by the way, is an excellent
technique to practice your creativity!)

When answering the question of "Who are you?" this
way, we have a hard time connecting with other people and
honestly, with ourselves. When you meet someone new, you
want to know who they really are (behind their business card).
That's how you create trust and connection, and it goes for any
kind of relationship. Therefore, knowing who you are can help
you build better relationships in all areas of your life.

Besides that, as humans, we all crave ways to get to know
ourselves better and to understand why we do what we do.
Knowing who you are helps you to connect with yourself:
past, present, and future. It helps you understand your passions and interests, and how to use them to achieve the goals
you set for yourself. We are more fulfilled and complete when
we know who we really are.

What if I had answered the question of, "Who are
you?" this way:

*Hi, my name is Diogo Seixas. I am a dreamer and a passion-
ate person who loves learning from life and from every experience.
I'm someone who is always going after my dreams and doing what
makes me feel good. I love my family and the people around me.*

I also live in the present and accept the fact that I'll be constantly changing. I'm curious and always looking for ways to improve. I know when to persist and when to give up. Nice to meet you!

See how much the two answers differ? One is totally based on the things I do and the other is based on who I actually am. The second answer is based on my current values: courage, love, consciousness, fulfilment, and progress. The questions now are, do you know who you are and what is important to you?

A key point to know is that not many people understand how to answer the "Who are you?" question properly, and the ones who do stand out from the rest. So, what kind of person do you want to be? Take a few moments to reflect and answer this question in your journal.

Think about it
Who are you *without* saying what you do?

What are values, and why do we use them?

My journey with values began a while ago, and for me, it is one of the most important things I have done regarding my life. The easiest way I can explain what a value is and how we can use them is to say that **a value is something that is important to you, and that guides your decisions and behaviors to create more experiences and better relationships in your life.**

The topic of values is interesting for a lot of people. We don't really *consciously* think about what we hold as important to us; we just know. When meeting with one of my students,

DIOGO SEIXAS

we talked about his first experience thinking about his own values. He told me it was so hard to put into words the things that matter to him. He kind of knew what they were, but when put on the spot, it was challenging for him to name them. If we don't consciously know what is important to us, don't you think it might be hard to make decisions?

In 2017, I was invited to leave Brazil and come to the U.S. to get my MBA while working as the coordinator of the Leadership Development Program. By this time, I was in a very good place in my personal and professional life. Our organization was starting to get good traction and was helping a lot of people in Brazil. We were doing great and getting involved with bigger and bigger events. The opportunity to get a free MBA and work for one of the best leadership programs in the U.S. was very tempting, but I was afraid that I would be doing the "wrong thing" by leaving Brazil and abandoning something that I was already happy doing.

After talking with my parents, mentors, and friends, I couldn't still figure out what I wanted to do. Then, I looked at my values and *at that time* (we will talk about this in one second) my number one value was contribution. Helping people and developing them in any way I could was the most important thing for me, so I pondered my decision based on that one value. It was hard to decide because I was living that value already in Brazil, but I also knew that accepting this opportunity would help me contribute to even more people in both countries. Knowing that information, it made sense for me to come to the US and begin a new journey.

Making this decision was very hard, but it became less painful because I knew what my values were and how making this decision would help me align more with those values. Relying on that knowledge helps me make better guided future-oriented decisions, decreasing the chances of some kind of frustration later on down the line. Values not only help us make better decisions, but they also help us to shape our behavior to create new habits, have better relationships, and give us that extra push toward the experiences we've been craving. Now, let's look a little more at the advantages of understanding our values.

#1 - Values can help us make better decisions

If you know what is important to you, you know how to make better decisions about your own future. In my story, knowing that my first value was "contribution" made the decision of coming to the U.S. much easier. If safety and stability were high on my list of values, my decision would probably have been different; I would've chosen to stay in Brazil, close to my family and doing something I was already good at and enjoyed.

If you don't know your values, you might spend a lot of time wondering about a decision and you probably encounter a lot of pain in the process. Even when you finally make a choice, you still may not be sure about it and won't be fully present during the aftermath. You might feel frustrated and uncertain throughout the whole decision-making process and even afterward.

For these reasons, knowing your values helps you to make smoother, conscious decisions (free of pain). Besides that, when you decide things based on your values, you decrease your chances of getting frustrated about the outcome of a decision because you will just be thinking about what is important to you.

Values help us make decisions, but before we can use them to choose our lives, we have to figure out what they are. Deciding upon your values gives you autonomy and control over your life. When you keep your values close as you plan for your future, you don't have to make decisions based on a gut feeling or on what other people tell you. Rather, you can decide based on what you truly think is important to you

Think about it

Think about a moment of indecision you have had in your life. Maybe it was a decision about your career, relationship, or education. Describe it and think about what kinds of values were involved in making that decision. Would acknowledging that some of your values are more important than others have helped you to make a better or less painful decision?

#2 - Values can shape our behaviors and habits

Before understanding how values could influence and help improve my life, I used to value "dreaming." For me, dreaming about the future was very important because it gave me the vision and direction I always needed. I was never a person who made things happen; I'm a very good strategist and thinker but was never great at taking ideas off of the paper and into reality.

At some point, I realized that if I didn't take my ideas off the paper, nothing would actually happen. I was leaving my life to destiny, and sometimes destiny is not very nice to us. I then decided to include the value "achievement" on the list of my top three values. This was a value that was previously somewhere (lower) on my list, but it wasn't one that I was giving focus or effort toward.

After moving achievement up on my list, I started to be more mindful about it. I brought it from my unconscious mind to my consciousness. I started telling people about it, and more importantly, finding ways to practice it. With these external changes I was creating in my life, my behaviors started changing as well. I looked for ways to put my ideas into practice and found people who could help me.

After starting Movement Journey, a lot had to change in my life. I was still in college, so I had to juggle many different responsibilities. My schedule was jam-packed with meetings, having classes almost every day with a few afternoons free, studying, homework, reading, and working out. It was hard to find the energy to take care of my education, business, and health all at the same time. What made a difference for me was the value I had at the top of my list, "contribution." I *had* to help people somehow, and to do that I had to adapt my routine. I started waking up earlier and organizing my day so I could do everything I both needed and wanted. Having a value at the forefront of my decision-making made a huge difference in the way I behaved.

When people tell me that they want to start waking up earlier or start a new habit of reading or exercising, the first thing I ask them is, "why?" I need to understand how important the change is for them. What value is behind the desire for that habit? **For any habit that needs to be created, a value needs to be found.** A value represents a need a person has to create some kind of change in their life.

> **Think about it**
> What are the habits you need to create or change? What kinds of new behaviors would you like to adopt into your daily life? Explore why you want them and what kind of value(s) could be behind your desires.

#3 - Values can increase the quality of our relationships

We briefly mentioned this when we were talking about the "Who are you?" question, and how answering it on a deeper level helps you to connect with other people. When you know your values and you communicate them to others, you increase your chances of having better relationships with them.

When you get to know someone's values on a deeper level, you get to know what is important to them. Knowing what is important to them helps you to understand what to do to develop your relationship. More importantly, it helps you understand what *not* to do so you don't screw things up with that person. Let's say that your best friend values honesty, for example. This means that your friend would rather hear the hard truth than a shallow lie.

When people communicate their values to each other, they are basically setting rules for the relationship. I'll tell you that love and respect is important, and you will tell me that happiness and communication are important. Based on that, we know better how to deal with each other. I know I have to over-communicate with you, and you know that you have to be caring and respectful toward me. When talking with someone, having their values in mind can help you know what to say and how to handle the conversation.

Think about romantic relationships; how would this idea come in handy in that realm? Many times we screw up because we simply don't know what is important to the other person. We always say, "I didn't know you cared so much about this." We have to have these discussions; they can make a world of difference. In my relationship, we have set the rules as to what values we have. Because of this, we more often know what to do and how to act toward one another in serious conversations. Even better, we hold each other accountable for the rules we set together and ensure that the relationship is on good terms.

Think about it

Is there a relationship with a friend, family member, or significant other that you would like to improve? What kind of values would you like to have in the relationship? Brainstorm with the other person and outline which values are important to both of you.

#4 - Values can shape our experiences

Looking into meaningful experiences you have had is a great way to find values. You can think about relationships you have had, jobs you've worked, and what you learned from either of them. Maybe you can think about that one time you tried to start your own business, for example. These experiences shape our values.

I remember when we started thinking and planning for Movimento Journey. One of our colleagues brought to our attention that, although we had a great background and experience from the Leadership Development Program, our development couldn't stop there; we should continue to learn and grow every day. He then showed a friend of his who was reading and participating in a bunch of training, and how that continuing education was really helping his business. This was a wake up call for me. Right after that, I started reading more and looking for other ways to develop myself, both personally and professionally. I looked at my values and decided to make growth one of them. Then, I decided I should learn something new every day and become better than what I was the day before. I carry that growth mindset to this day. The reality check from my colleague changed my mindset and helped me to incorporate growth as one of my most prioritized values.

In the same way that our experiences shape our values, our values also shape our experiences. When you choose something to care about because it will help you to get closer to your desired future, you will also start seeking out experiences to live that value. And guess what? Every experience you seek will affirm your value, turning into a virtuous cycle of positive reinforcement.

When I decided to become a speaker, I was very afraid of what other people would think about me. Being on stage and doing videos and podcasts was very hard because all I could think about was what others were thinking. Would they make fun of me? Would they think that what I had to say was good and relevant? What if I fail; are people going to support me or laugh? After spending a while thinking these anxious thoughts, I reflected on my values and decided that I needed something powerful to create a new mindset for myself in this realm. I resignified my value of contribution, where it now meant helping anyone, no matter whom. If I gave a speech to 200 people, all that mattered was that one person left the event with something new in mind and with energy to do more.

My goal wasn't to please everybody, but help someone. This really changed my attitude toward putting myself out there. I started doing more online content because my focus was on that one person rather than the entire crowd. The choice of what to care about and the meaning I gave to that helped me seek more experiences to reassure my value.

The secret to all of this is to understand what is important to you based on your choices or the experiences you have had. When we make even these micro-changes in our value systems, little by little, we become the people we want to be.

> **Think about it**
> Go back to the lifeline exercise and take a look at the experiences that made who you are. How can you transform them into values? In other words, how can translate what you have learned into a value that you can carry on?

The hierarchy

Based on what we saw previously, knowing our values helps us to make better decisions. It also helps to guide our behavior. If these things are true, why is it that even when we know our values, making decisions is still really hard? Every indecision is a conflict of values. Think about your two favorite hobbies in the whole world. If I were to ask you to choose just one, how hard would that be? So, what if you decided before you came upon a decision, which value was most important to you? Wouldn't that make things easier?

It's not enough to just know what you value, it's also important to know what value you hold closest to you. Deciding between adventure and security might be hard since they are opposites, but if you know which is more important for you *right now*, the choice will be less painful. Think about deciding between love and success. Sometimes people need to decide between moving to a different city and being away from the love of their life or staying where they are and passing up a great opportunity somewhere else. It is a painful decision, but knowing which value is most important for you helps in the process.

Please, understand that I am not advocating for you to choose one OR the other. When we talk about values, it is more like a temporary concession. One value may be a priority, but the other is not excluded. In the success and love case, making a choice to take the new opportunity doesn't mean that you have to break up with your significant other. Since the value attached to the opportunity is prioritized higher for you, your relationship will just have to adapt (communication is very important in this situation!).

You may have realized by now that each time I talk about values, I start with "at the time, x was important to me." This is because values change over time. You live different things and your priorities change. Therefore, what is important to you will change as well. Don't think that you are immutable, because as you learned earlier, you changed from three years ago, one year ago, maybe even since you started reading this book!

Family was something that was always very important to me. However, at the time that I had to make the decision of whether to move to the U.S., my contribution value was higher in the hierarchy than my family value. This doesn't mean that family was not important to me anymore, but at that time in my life, contribution was *more* important. Besides that, I knew that my family would be happy if I was contributing and helping people as well.

The important takeaway here is that you need to know the order of your values. This will help you make better decisions with less pain, and also help you prioritize what is most important to you in that moment of your life.

Exercise - Finding your core values

Now that you know some benefits of having values and how they can help you on your path, I want you to think about ten values you possess in your life today. What are the ten most important things for you? Below, you will find a sample list of values you can use for reference, though if you have others, use them! When doing this exercise, also think about the other exercises we've done so far; you may be able to find valuable information about what you value in those as well.

Accountability	Collaboration	Dignity
Achievement	Commitment	Diversity
Adaptability	Community	Environment
Adventure	Compassion	Efficiency
Altruism	Competence	Equality
Ambition	Confidence	Ethics
Authenticity	Connection	Excellence
Balance	Contentment	Fairness
Beauty	Contribution	Faith
Being the best	Cooperation	Family
Belonging	Courage	Financial stability
Career	Creativity	Forgiveness
Caring	Curiosity	Freedom

Friendship	Joy	Reliability
Fun	Justice	Respect
Generosity	Kindness	Responsibility
Giving back	Knowledge	Risk-taking
Grace	Leadership	Security
Gratitude	Learning	Self-discipline
Growth	Legacy	Self-respect
Harmony	Leisure	Service
Health	Love	Spirituality
Honesty	Loyalty	Stewardship
Hope	Nature	Success
Humility	Openness	Teamwork
Humor	Optimism	Trust
Inclusion	Order	Truth
Independence	Parenting	Understanding
Initiative	Patience	Usefulness
Integrity	Patriotism	Vision
Intuition	Perseverance	Vulnerability
Job security	Recognition	

What are your values?

1. _____   6. _____

2. _____   7. _____

3. _____   8. _____

4. _____   9. _____

5. _____   10. _____

The secret about values

In past chapters, we have talked about setting a direction and goals for your life. The secret about values is that we can use them to help us achieve the goals we set for ourselves. Think about it, if values shape our decisions and behaviors to create better experiences and relationships, we can choose powerful values that will influence and help us achieve our goals.

Another reason why our values need some deliberate choosing is because people tend to adopt **limiting values**. If you have a value like "patience," but have a goal of becoming the CEO of a big company, your goal may never be achieved because your value will limit the actions you can take to get closer to that goal. When we set values, we need to ask ourselves, **"What values do I need to have to achieve the future I want?"** It's much more effective to set values when you know what you want to achieve.

People may wonder if choosing their values would feel forced or against their nature and who they are. I'm not asking you to choose *only* values that will pump up your actions; a person can't only live from growth, achievement, determination, progress, and success. One of those would be great to give you some motivation, but holding all of those as critical to your being would definitely stress you out. The key is to find the values that can help you get closer to your dreams but that are still true to who you are.

In the next chapter, we will be talking about how the definitions of our values influence and impact our lives. You can still have a value for achievement, for example, but it may not have anything to do with money. It might be something health-or people-related. For now, I want you to think about your values, choose which values will help you in the future, and be clear about a general definition you assign to them.

Think about it

Looking at your future and the goals you want to achieve in the next three years, what would you change from your values list? Would you add anything? Would you remove anything? Do you think you have any limiting values? Take a look again and make the proper adjustments, but don't worry too much about the order right now. We will get into something a little bit more complex for this soon. What are the values you need to possess in order to achieve the future you want?

Your updated list of values:

1. _____   6. _____

2. _____   7. _____

3. _____   8. _____

4. _____   9. _____

5. _____   10. _____

Exercise - The Prioritizing Grid

All right, now that you have your updated list of values, we will use a different process to prioritize them. Let's take a deeper look at the relationship that each value has with the others. I like to call this a "Value Battle." You will find the grid on the following page. You can also find a copy online using the following link: www.rideacad.com/resources. Here is how you will use the grid:

Step 01: Add your ten updated values (in no specific order) in the "List of Values" column.

Step 02: Here is where the fun starts. Let's say that your first, second, and third values are courage, family, and success, respectively. In the "Values Battle" section, you will see many "number vs. number" squares. Let's use as an example 1 vs. 2. We will start by challenging the values of "courage" and "family." Which one is more important to you? Let's say that you choose courage because you know that your family wants you to be brave and do the things you want in your life. In this case, we will be circling the number 1 in the square, showing that the courage won the battle.

I would recommend going down by columns. Therefore, the next battle would be between values 1 (courage) and 3 (success). Which one is more important? Let's say that you choose courage again, since to be successful, you need to find the courage to put your ideas into practice. Circle the number 1 again in the second square of the first column. Follow this process with all of the other columns.

Step 03: We will be counting and organizing the value battles. In the values line on the bottom part of the table, you will have numbers from 1 to 10 that represent the values in the "List of Values" column. In the following line, insert how many times you circled each number in the values battle. For example, if I circled courage (number 1) four times, family (number 2) one time, success (number 3) zero times, love (number 4) three times, and contribution (number 5) two times, I will insert those numbers below the respective value number. You will see that all number ones are in one column, but the number fours are spread half in the column and half on the line.

Step 04: In the prioritized list of values, you will just rewrite your new list based on the bottom row from Step 03.

LIST OF VALUES

Step 01: Insert your initial list below. Write down 10 different values. Don't worry about the order yet.

1	
2	
3	
4	
5	
6	
7	
8	
9	
10	

VALUES BATTLE

Step 02: Here is where the battle of values happen. You will compare each one of the values and circle which one is more important to you.

1 vs 2								
1 vs 3	2 vs 3							
1 vs 4	2 vs 4	3 vs 4						
1 vs 5	2 vs 5	3 vs 5	4 vs 5					
1 vs 6	2 vs 6	3 vs 6	4 vs 6	5 vs 6				
1 vs 7	2 vs 7	3 vs 7	4 vs 7	5 vs 7	6 vs 7			
1 vs 8	2 vs 8	3 vs 8	4 vs 8	5 vs 8	6 vs 8	7 vs 8		
1 vs 9	2 vs 9	3 vs 9	4 vs 9	5 vs 9	6 vs 9	7 vs 9	8 vs 9	
1 vs 10	2 vs 10	3 vs 10	4 vs 10	5 vs 10	6 vs 10	7 vs 10	8 vs 10	9 vs 10

	1	2	3	4	5	6	7	8	9
VALUES — Numbers from your initial list of values									
BATTELS WON — **Step 03:** Count how many times you circled each value and insert the number in the corresponding column									

PRIORITIZED LIST OF VALUES

Step 04: Based on how many times you circled each value, re-write your list in order from the most circled, to the least

1	
2	
3	
4	
5	
6	
7	
8	
9	
10	

Created by the RIDE Academy
www.rideacad.com

159

You just created your compass

Congratulations, you just created your personal compass for decision-making and habit changing! However, we are not done yet, and there will be more work to do in the following chapters. Updating your values is creating a way to live your life by design. You get to decide what your goals are and what is important to you.

Personally, I review my values every six months. Think about how many experiences you gain in six months. There can be big changes that some of those experiences call for; what we experience shapes who we are, the way we think, and the things that are important to us. Don't be afraid to revisit this exercise whenever you need.

Essentially, what we are working to do here is take things from our unconscious minds and bring it to our conscious minds. We have thought about our goals and values, and now we will be thinking about ways we can live our values, developing actions that will help us to get closer and closer to our ideal lives. We are going through this process consciously and will practice it consciously. Like everything though, after a while, it will become a habit. We will transform the actions we are deliberately taking now into unconscious behavior.

Takeaways

When we define ourselves by what we do, we have a hard time connecting with other people and honestly, with ourselves. When you meet someone new, you want to know who they really are (behind their business card).

A value is something that is important to you, and that guides your decisions and behaviors to create more experiences and better relationships in your life.

Knowing your values helps you to make smoother, conscious decisions (free of pain). When you decide things based on your values, you decrease your chances of getting frustrated about the outcome of a decision because you will just be thinking about what is important to you.

For any habit that needs to be created, a value needs to be found. A value represents a need a person has to create some kind of change in their life.

When you get to know someone's values on a deeper level, you get to know what is important to them. Knowing what is important to them helps you to understand what to do to develop your relationship

In the same way our experiences shape our values, our values also shape our experiences. When you choose something to care about because it will help you get closer to your future, you will start seeking out experiences to live that value.

It's not enough to just know what you value, it's also important to know what value you hold closest to you.

The secret about values is that we can use them to help us achieve the goals we set for ourselves. If values shape our decisions and behaviors to create better experiences and relationships, we can choose powerful values that will influence and help us achieve our goals.

CHAPTER 11

How To Practice My Values

What's the meaning behind your values?

Everything in life is about the meaning we give to it. As you might suspect by now, it isn't much different with our values. It's very easy to get confused about what someone means by their values. When someone says that dedication is their number one value, for example, there are many different interpretations for that. Does this person mean they work tirelessly all the time? Does it mean that they are the first to get to the office in the morning and the last to leave at night? Does it mean that they never give up on challenges? If you understand what someone means by their values, it will be easier to understand how they will behave and how you can behave in relation to them.

The challenge is that there is a communicative disconnect when we don't understand people's reasons for their values. We give our own ideas to other people's values when we are unsure of what they mean, and very often the meanings we attach are extremely different compared to the true reasons. We have different definitions than other people for love, family, dedication, and happiness, and if we don't communicate this, we might have a conflict in values. Actually, any kind of conflict is nothing more than a conflict of values. For that reason, it's very important to communicate what you mean about your values, and ask what others mean by theirs. The names you give to your values are only 20% of the process. The other 80% is about the meaning you give to them.

Communicating what your values are and mean to the people around you can increase the quality of any relationship of which you are a part. Think about the following situation: You and your partner both value love. That is a great thing, right? Not quite. What if your definition of love means support and encouragement, and that whatever you do, you will give support to and expect support from your partner? What if to your partner, love means physical contact, texting, and talking all the time? Think now about when it comes time to make that decision between taking that big promotion in a different city or staying in the same place professionally. Will you face a challenge? Definitely! Because you want support from your partner and they want to be close to you.

So again, not only communicating your values, but also what you mean by them is crucial in any relationship, romantic or otherwise. I've said it before but here it is again: Every conflict between people is a conflict of values. Think about conflicts regarding the environment, capitalism, communism, politics, health, etc. Having a different opinion just means that you value different things than the other person. We often wonder why it is so hard to change people's minds; it's because when you are trying to do this, you are basically asking them to give up their belief about something important to them and care about what you want instead. How closed-minded is this!?

Every time you have a discussion with someone where you have conflicting opinions, never take it personally. You value different things. Always think about the relationship you have with that person. Ask yourself, "is it really worth it to damage our relationship because of this conflict?" We need to be ready to adapt, and to sometimes make a concession of values. In other words, be ready to give up some of your beliefs for the greater good of your relationships.

Besides increasing the quality of your relationships, giving meaning to your values helps you understand what you have to do to live and practice them, especially when you can translate their meanings into actions. For a good portion of this chapter, we will see how we can do this by creating rules for your values.

Think about it

What are some of the relationships you have where you can share your values and ask for the other person's values?

What are rules?

I learned the concept of rules in relation to values for the first time from Tony Robbins. **A rule is a condition, action, or event that needs to happen so you know that you are living out your value.** In a more simplistic way, a rule is the definition you give to your values, which very often is translated into actions that you can follow.

Let's say you want to have a great career as an entrepreneur and, for that, growth might be an important value to you. Some rules you can have for growth are to read books about entrepreneurship, go to events to learn more about it, or maybe interviewing entrepreneurs so you can get to know and learn from them. You are not growing your business yet, but you know what to do to get closer to that future based on your value of growth. Those are ways that you can live your value growth, based on your goal of wanting to become an entrepreneur. When defining your rules, here are some things to be aware of:

- A rule must be **actionable:** If your value is health, an actionable rule is to run five miles a week or to eat a healthy meal every other day. A bad example would be to lose five pounds: "I'll know I am living my value of health when I lose five pounds." This is more like an actual goal and a consequence of the rules you set. Rules must be something you can start doing *right now*.

- You must have **control** over your rules: If your value is happiness, you can't set a rule that says every time someone hugs you or tells how much you matter to them will be a good way to live this value. You don't have control over what other people do; you can only control yourself. To be happy, a rule could be to send gratitude letters or tell people how much they matter to you.

- A rule must be **tangible:** Find things you can do daily. Let's say you have a value called "fun." If you tell me that you live this value by travelling the world, this won't happen very often (I assume) and therefore you won't be living this value enough. This could lead to you feeling bad about it. However, if you set a rule like "When my partner and I get out of the house for dinner..." or "When I do something out of my routine...," these are closer to your reality. You can do them any time.

An easy way you can go about creating your rules is to complete the sentence:

I know I'm living in (x value) when_(rule)_happens.

I'll give you a personal example using one of my current values and rules. Before I talk about my most important value, the number one on my hierarchy list, "courage," I will give you some context so you understand the rules I created. In May of 2020, I had to rediscover somehow reinvent myself. I was transitioning from my old job to the PhD program I'm in now and I was feeling kind of lost about what I actually wanted to do with my life.

I remember feeling a lot of pain during this period. I was confused about what to do next. This was incredibly hard for me, because I had always known what to do and was excellent at helping people figure out their next steps as well. But there I was, lost and incapable of describing what I was feeling. I remember looking at social media, seeing everybody do such many amazing things and feeling very overwhelmed. Just to give you a little context, this all happened when COVID-19 was exploding, so you might remember the amount of free content that was available online. Yet there I was, doing nothing.

Because of all those feelings, I knew I had to explore something deeper within myself. I decided to stop looking outside and look a little more inside of who I was. That's when I began to explore my values and try to understand more of what was going on. Thanks to that action, I learned a few things about myself and what I thought was important. First, stopping my work of helping people, which I had been doing for quite some time, was totally against my value of "contribution," and that explained why I was feeling so bad. I wasn't doing something that was important to me. I was always used to putting others before myself, and had this excessive goal of helping to improve other people's lives. However, at the time I was going through this, I was experiencing an identity crisis of sorts; I wasn't helping people anymore and that was causing me a lot of pain. After coming to this realization, I started questioning whether contribution as a value aligned with that period in my life. I started thinking about my goals and the things I needed to get done, and concluded that my goal in the moment was to get clear about what I wanted to do with my life and what would make me feel happy.

I decided that, for the time being, I needed to remove contribution from the top of my list. For someone who is used to helping people, it takes a lot of courage to put yourself first. Because of this, I knew that I needed to add courage to my list. When reflecting about my secondary goals, I realized that I always did things other people told me to do: write more, make videos, listen to podcasts, create social media content. Some of those activities brought me pleasure, but some didn't. I began to recognize that I did them anyway because they were what others wanted me to do, and since I had to help them (because of my value of "contribution"), I followed their instructions. Not only did reviewing my values lead me to shifting what mattered to me, but it also showed me how I had let my values move me to do things that made me unhappy.

That's around the same time I heard an episode of Brene's Brown podcast where she interviewed Alicia Keys. I remember Alicia saying that the turn-around of her career happened when she stopped making songs because others liked them and started making songs that she liked instead. Rather than writing for people, she wrote for herself. That helped her to feel better about herself and her work because it was more authentic. I decided I wanted that, too.

Finally, in those moments of my life, I was comfortable with where I was and that bugged me. I had a steady job, was making decent money, and felt secure. Those are all great things, but I was 28 at the time and I had always told myself that I would be willing to take risks and make mistakes for as long as I could. I was missing something new, something exciting, something unstable. Somewhere along the way, I got used to stability and put my dreams aside. I knew I had to change that; I knew I didn't want that.

Making changes once you have gotten comfortable is not easy, and they will definitely not happen from one day to the next. The process starts with you thinking about what you want to change in the life you live every day. After all this reflection, I removed contribution from my value list and, between others, added the value "courage." Here are the rules I created for this value:

I know I experience **courage** when...

- I put myself first;
- I do what makes me feel good instead of what makes others feel good;
- I go after my dreams.

Setting rules

Right now, you have 10 values in order of priority. Before we start creating the rules for them, I have an extra challenge for you. Humans, naturally, have a hard time remembering things and even a harder time trying to focus on more than one thing at a time. This means that you will have a hard time trying to remember your ten values, and an even harder time making them all important at the same time.

To make this next exercise easier and more effective for you, I would recommend just focusing on five values. You might have to make some adjustments on your list of values, and that is okay. Maybe you're asking right now, "Why did I just come up with ten values instead of five?" I wanted you to be sure about what's most important for you, and even though sometimes it's easier to go straight to five, we might be losing important reflections when we pick out only five values right away instead of ten. I wanted this to be hard in the beginning so you could be sure certain things were really important to you.

Therefore, from the ten values you listed, narrow down to five. You don't need to use the grid again, this can be more based on how you feel about what to keep and what to give up. You can choose the first five and cut off the last five. You can mix some values together or incorporate some of them as rules for some other value.

When I did this last time, I had values like progress, growth, creativity and persistence, ranking 5th, 6th, 7th, and 10th, respectively. I decided to include most of those values inside the value "progress." All of my initial values were still important for me and I wasn't ready to let them go. When looking at them all, progress seemed to be the most important and one that could encompass some others, so I found a way to bring them all together. Here are my rules for **progress**:

I experience **progress** when:

- I look at things with new eyes;
- I look for ways to grow and improve;
- I know when to persist and when to give up.

Exercise - Creating your rules

Think about your five new five values and think about what kind of rules you can create from your values. Remember to create rules that are actionable, controllable, tangible, and future-oriented. What kind of actions can you attach to your values that will help you to get closer to your goals?

I would recommend creating three rules per value. You can follow the script of "I experience my value X when Y happens," with X being a value and Y being the action. Another useful tip is to create actions that are oriented to your goals, like in the entrepreneur example. You can use your journal for now, or the workbook to this guide, available online.

Rules are the way to happiness

I want you to understand that through rules, we create ways to be happy. If you tell me that achievement is an important value to you and that to live this value you will create a rule where you need to write 3,000 words per week, that means you are setting yourself up to be happy when you get those 3,000 words done. For you, this action is doable and you are in control, you can start doing it right now. Following the rule helps you to live out something important to you, something that will give you happiness when you get it done. At the same time, following the rule should give you happiness during the process. Rules are the actions we create to make ourselves happy in the process of achieving our goals. They are how we make our journeys much more fulfilling.

I want you to think about how much thought you are currently putting into your life . In previous chapters, you decided the areas you wanted to focus on and the goals you had for them. You also created your values list by deciding what's important to you, and then you created rules to transform those important things into actions that will help you get you closer to your dreams. It's a very strategic and future-oriented process; kudos to you!

This is what we call living by design. You are not just waiting for life to throw something at you so you can react. You are being proactive about living life. You are proactively thinking about your goals and directing your decisions and habits to make the life you want happen. I want you to understand that you are in control of your life right now and you can create amazing things. You are not just in control of your future, but you are also in control of your present. You are deciding to be happy. That's the power of taking action toward your values.

How to sustain your values

We talked before about putting the importance of putting things into practice. The techniques and tools you will see next are ways to bring your values to the conscious world, and after practicing enough, they will become rooted in your mind. Therefore, good habits will help you get closer to your goals. Here are things that you can and should start doing right now to practice the new rules you've created:

Put them in a visible place

The first and most important step is to put your values in a visible place. No matter what you try, you need to put your values in a place where you will easily see them every day. I remember my chemistry teacher once saying that we should put the periodic table on our closet door or on the top of our bunk beds so we could always look at it and remember the elements. I'm now here asking you to do the same but with your values!

Personally, I do this in two ways. I have my top five values and their rules written on sticky notes and stuck to the wall in front of my work table. I'm staring at them (or they are staring at me) right now while I write this book. Having them here helps me to remember them all the time, especially when I'm reviewing my week in my journal. I look at my values and reflect when and how I lived my values during that week.

My journal is another way I keep track of my values. Since I'm not always home, but always have my journal, I can look at them whenever I need. They are written on the two last pages of all of my journals. The cool thing about this is that every time I get a new journal (every five or six months), I get the chance to take a look at my values and evaluate if they are still aligned with my goals and priorities.

To make your values visual, you can also write them on a piece of paper and keep it inside your wallet or make them your screensaver on your phone or desktop. You can be more specific and strategic, setting some values near the actions you need to take to live them out. You can put a sticky note in front of your fridge with your value of health with a rule to eat healthy. You could put another one close to your books with your value of growth/learning.

You can get as creative as you want here. The important thing is just to make your values visible in some way so you don't forget them and you can start to consciously practice them when you see them.

Talk to people about your values

Remember the first question I posed when we were talking about values? "Who are you without telling what you do?" What if you tried to answer that question more often? Think about this: If you were in a job interview and they asked you to talk about yourself, would you answer by talking about your values? What if you could use that same answer in your relationships? Think of how much you would impress people. You would be building better relationships while also practicing your values.

Talking about your values is a way to bring them to reality. The more often we talk about them, the clearer they get for us. We can talk about them when we get to know new people or even when we need to justify some decision we just made. If people ever question your attitudes toward something, explaining your opinion based on the values you hold might be very helpful. It will also set an example of who you are. People will be impressed knowing that you live your life by design instead of doing things just because you have no other choice.

Practice a value each week

Another interesting technique when you are trying to adapt to your new values is to choose one value each week to live consciously. Let's say you value progress like I do. To live this value, I need to consciously look for ways to improve. As you know, I'm always tracking my progress in different areas of life. I started this by running. I made a goal to improve my time, distance, or pace on every run. Each day, I had to do something better. I keep track of the number of pages I read, the number of words I write, and even the number of TV shows I watch.

The idea is to choose one of your top values and, throughout the week, find ways to live it out. When you finish your trial week, choose a different value and practice again. The secret here is the same thing we've said before. We are trying to take from the unconscious mind and bring into the conscious world. Practicing each of our values helps us to be more mindful about ways that we can incorporate them into our daily routines.

Evaluate your values

This is an excellent practice, especially at the beginning of your values journey. We talked in one of the first chapters about the importance of having a journal. You can evaluate every week the progress you are making on living out your values. If you are applying the previous technique and practicing one value a week, ask yourself at the end of the week how well you lived that value and what you could've done better, then track your progress over time.

If you are past that initial phase, you can continue evaluating your values every week. You might ask yourself what values you intend to practice in the next week and which ones you could've done a better job practicing the week before. No matter what, you want to keep improving the way you consciously live out your values. Remember, if you do that, you are basically keeping track of the ways you can be happier.

More than just evaluating your values on a weekly basis, don't forget that you can also re-do everything once in a while. Like I said earlier, I review my values every time I get a new journal. About every six months, I get the opportunity to look at my goals and at the things that are important to me. During this time, I can evaluate my direction, my priorities, and the actions I need to take to connect the two. I think about new values, re-do the prioritizing grid, reduce my top values to five and create new rules if I need.

Gauge your decision based on your values

Another way you can practice your values is to consciously use them when you need to decide something. Remember when I had to decide about my future, whether I should stay in Brazil and keep my project going or come to the U.S. to get my MBA and work for the LDP? I made that decision consciously based on my values.

When faced with moments of uncertainty, take a look at the options available to solve your problem and evaluate how well each option fits your values. In my case, between the option of challenging myself in the U.S. or the option of staying in Brazil, the first one made more sense based on my value of contribution. Try to be more conscious about the big decisions you have to make by looking at what is important to you.

Your bad days are the days you don't live your values

I bet you have had bad days in your life. Those might be the days you can't find motivation anywhere and everything might be really hard to do. Very recently, I had a day like this. I woke up a little off and couldn't figure out why. I started to doubt myself and all the bad thoughts about not being enough started to flood my brain. I spent the day in bed, watching TV shows. I ate extremely poorly, had a few drinks, did not exercise at all, and spent the whole day in a bad mood.

Later that night I got tired of feeling like that and got up to write about my day. I keep this practice of journaling about things pretty often. For me, it's like talking to myself. As soon as I sat down to write, I looked at my values and realized I hadn't practiced any of them the entire day. I had actually done pretty much the opposite; I did lots of things that did not align with my values. It's no wonder why I felt so bad throughout the day.

That's when I had one of my biggest insights about values. The same way living our values makes us happy, not living our values makes us unhappy. I know it sounds very trivial right now, but it couldn't be more true. The takeaway here is that when you are having a bad day, take a look at your values and see if there is anything you can do that will help you live one of them out. This will help you to get back on track, get you feeling happy, and put you back in a better mood.

> **Think about it**
> Think about a recent bad day you had. Did you live your values? Were you practicing any of them that day?

Now, it's up to you

I'm extremely biased about the power of values. I can't even say how much value work helps me every day. It helps me to guide my everyday decisions about my future. I feel like I've never been as in control of my own life as I am today. Of course, everyone still has their bad days, but that's the wake up call we need to look back at our values. There might be something wrong, or it can just be a way to bring your mind back to what makes you feel good.

Every time I need a new habit or a change in life, I look to my values and find ways that they can help me. Today I understand the *value of the values*. People don't always understand this and they underestimate how being conscious about what is important to you can change your life. Don't be one of those people! You learned how just this simple process can help you to take control over your life. Now it's up to you to make it happen.

Takeaways

🔑 Communicating what your values are and mean to the people around you can increase the quality of any relationship of which you are a part.

- Giving meaning to your values helps you understand what you have to do to live and practice them, especially when you can translate their meanings into actions.

- A rule is the definition you give to your values, which very often is translated into actions that you can follow.

- The same way living our values makes us happy, not living our values makes us unhappy. I know it sounds very trivial right now, but it couldn't be more true. The takeaway here is that when you are having a bad day, take a look at your values and see if there is anything you can do that will help you live one of them out.

CHAPTER 12

How To Be Happier

The Genie Question

Think about this: What if a genie showed up right now and gave you three wishes? There are no restrictions at all; you can ask for whatever you need. What would your three wishes be?

Wish #1: _____

_____

Wish #2: _____

_____

Wish #3: _____

_____

I saw this question in the book, *"If You're So Smart, Why aren't You Happy?"* by Raj Raghunathan. Raj asked this question in his classes and noted that only 18 to 30 percent of his students had happiness on their lists. I'm someone who loves to do those kinds of experiments myself, so I started asking this question in my speeches, trainings, and coach meetings. Raj is right.

I got a wide variety of answers when I asked my students this question: cars, houses, financial stability, family, kids, time travel, the ability to see the future, the ability to heal the world, or the ability to read minds. Don't get me wrong, all of those are valuable wishes, and I bet if you didn't write something similar on your own list, you want to go back and re-do the exercise.

Sure, this exercise is fun, but the important thing here is that very few people choose happiness as one of their wishes. A lot of people don't believe it is possible to achieve happiness right now. Not many have it as a **conscious goal**. The reason why I say happiness is not a conscious goal is because people chose the other things as wishes, thinking that in the end, if they got those things, they would be happy. People think about happiness as something that we get *through* something else, rather than something we can consciously aim for and achieve right now.

Think about that for a second. You are always delaying your happiness and conditioning it to something, or even worse, someone. We keep transferring dreams: "When I get married, I'll do this," "When I get money, I'll do that," or "When I leave college, I'll do something else." We are always postponing our dreams instead of doing them *right now*. The problem is that, the older we get, the harder it will be to focus on a dream or single thing that you are very passionate about. Life happens, people happen, bills happen, kids happen, along with everything else being alive brings us. Things will always happen. How do we handle this?

The truth is that even when we achieve that *one thing* we really want, we get used to it and start wishing for the next thing. This is called "hedonic adaptation," and it is what happens when you are very excited about your new phone, for example, but after a while, you get used to it and it just becomes part of your life. We get used to something that once excited us. Fun fact: this happens with relationships as well. Life satisfaction levels for married couples start coming back down to the same levels as before the wedding, two to three years after the event occurs.

So, how can we be more mindful about our own happiness <u>and</u> focus on what we have *instead* of what we wish we had? There are many techniques that we will talk about, but for now I just want you to know that happiness is something that you can and should start pursuing today. It's not about the past, it's not about the future, but it's about what is happening right now. You have control over your *right now*. A phrase that stuck with me from the book *Happiness by Design* from Paul Dolan is that "happiness lost today is happiness for forever", so let's not waste time and be happy.

Be grateful

Gratitude is important because it shifts our focus. We are so used to complaining and looking at what is wrong with life that we forget to look at things in a positive light. If we can look at the things we have and be grateful for them, our energy and focus will be on what makes us happy instead of what may be lacking. Gratitude is something that takes practice; for some people it comes naturally, but other people really struggle with it.

One of the best exercises I've ever done for gratitude was writing a letter to someone who had impacted my life. I ended up thanking so many people because I realized that I wouldn't be where I am if it weren't for any of them.

Celina Alves was the president of AIESEC in Uberlândia when we first started AIESEC in Uberaba in 2013. She was the one who challenged me to do my first presentation in front of a group of people outside the classroom. My friend Camila Venturolli landed me the DVD box of the TV show *Friends*, from which I learned a lot of English—and about life in general. My little brother, Henrique, is teaching me how to be persistent and brave. My parents taught me the importance of being friendly and of understanding that although life might be hard, we will always have each other and everything will always be okay. Those are just a few examples of the many gratitude letters, thank you notes, text and Facebook messages I sent to people to thank them for helping me to become the person I am today.

When doing this exercise, you will think about what things and which people made you who you are. Just by thinking about this, you will become happier. And guess what? When you recognize and thank people for impacting your life, you make them happy, too. You can even encourage others to do this exercise as well, starting the positivity cycle we all need.

There are other ways to practice gratitude. You can use your journal to write things for which you are grateful. I've done this in both daily and weekly increments. The good thing about gratitude practice is that after a while, you start going more in-depth. You might start on the first day by being grateful for family, food, and shelter, but after a while you learn how to look at life with new eyes and be thankful for the sun, the trees, and animals for their role in nature.

> **Think about it**
> What are the things that you are grateful for or the people whom you are grateful for in your life? Write about them in your journal and, if you want to make someone happy, tell them about the impact they have had on your life so far.

Define happiness

We have talked extensively in this book about meaning, and here we are again. This is one of the big ones for me. A lot of people don't even think about defining happiness, and when they do is very superficial or in material terms. The key to being happier is to define happiness as something achievable that you can easily access.

The way you define happiness is related to the way you feel about happiness. You can define happiness by being able to do things like travel the world, make a lot of money, or be famous. It's okay, that's your choice. The way I see happiness is by being around the ones I love or to see them doing well. I'm also happy when I'm doing something I like and helping others at the same time. These are things that I can do every day and, as a result, I can feel happy every day.

Think about what "being happy" means to you. What are the things that make you happy in your daily life? What are the things that you most often take for granted? The gift of waking up, having food on the table, having enough money to get by, good parents, a supportive family, funny friends, a healthy relationship, those are all good reasons for someone to be happy. Think about the way you see happiness and it will change the way you feel about it.

How expectations are related to happiness

Just for a second, think about what you are satisfied about in your life and why. Let's use as an example someone who is satisfied with his relationship because he has a partner who is always willing to talk to him and share the highs and lows of life. He is also satisfied because they both make a conscious effort to love each other and are committed to making each other happy.

Now, think about things that you are not satisfied about in your life. What are they? As an example, I will use someone who is not satisfied with her career because she always thought she would be further along by the age she is now. She is not happy with her boss, who keeps putting pressure on her and stops her from doing creative work.

It turns out that your life satisfaction is extremely related to your expectations about life. When your expectations are being met, you are happy. When they aren't, you are not happy. That's why it's not just the definition you give to happiness that's important, it's what you do to close the gap between your definition and your feelings. For the first person in our example, his expectation of a healthy relationship is something where both partners share love and happiness and communicate super well. Because that happens in his relationship, he is happy. In the second example, she wants a boss who will let her be creative and autonomous. She also had expected to be further in her career by now. Because her expectations are not being met, she is unhappy.

Tony Robbins uses this concept to explain that, basically, to feel happy, you need to either alter your expectations or work on bringing your life situation to meet the expectations you currently have. In the second example, if the woman is unhappy with her career, she has the option to either lower her expectations and see what good comes from the job she currently has or work on bringing her career up to her higher expectation. Maybe, if she is in the finance world, she can redefine the meaning of her job to say that she helps people make their dreams come true by rearranging their finances. . If she is in finance and wants to be further along in her career, she might think about getting another degree or completing some leadership training to climb higher at work.

I haven't seen many cases where we need to lower our expectations, although that does happen sometimes! The main problem is when people have high expectations but don't do anything to make their realities match. If you tell me you want to be a CEO, but you watch TV all day and don't know anything about business or entrepreneurship, the gap between your expectation and your reality gets bigger and bigger with each passing minute. Expectations and actions must be aligned so you can feel more satisfied with your life.

Think about it

What are the things in your life with which you are not satisfied right now? What is the expectation, and what are you doing to fill the gap? Can you do anything differently today? What are the actions you need to start taking immediately?

Being present

I remember a day when I had to travel to a city three hours from mine in Brazil. On the way home I had a truck in front of me that was moving very slowly. It was hard for me to pass it because it was a two-way road with only one lane on each side. For about 20 minutes I was behind that truck, just waiting for the best time to pass in the safest manner. I was getting super irritated just as I went over a bridge. It was around 5pm, so the sun was setting and you could see the beautiful reflection in the water below.

Instantly, I felt peace.

I forgot about the truck for a bit and just focused on the view. I rolled down the windows, cranked the volume of whatever music was playing, and felt complete for just a second. I felt the wind on my face and the nice music in the background, and I appreciated the view for about 30 seconds. Thirty seconds totally changed my mood.

As soon as I got off the bridge, I thought about how awesome the experience had been for me and how good I felt for that half a minute. I had actually missed many amazing sights on the road just because I was so focused on the truck. Right then, it hit me:

That's life!

In life, sometimes we are so focused on an important goal ahead of us that we forget about the present moment. We forget about the things that we are experiencing right now. The worst part is that once I passed the first truck, there was another one ahead of it! It's the same with our goals; we keep pursuing one goal and when we finally achieve it, there is another one just ahead. And in racing to catch your goals, you might be missing a lot of what is happening in your *right now*.

Being present is one of the biggest gifts we can give ourselves. Pay attention to the little things around us: the colors, the sounds, the way our bodies feel, the experiences with our loved ones, the food, the animals… everything you can. Being present helps you to be less anxious about the future and less depressed about the past. Focus on what you can control—the present.

Paulo Vieira, a Brazilian author and life coach, helps us to understand three kinds of mentalities and how each one can have a big impact on us. Each one represents ways that we spend time in our lives, and how we split that time thinking about the past, the present or the future.

In the first scenario, called the depression model, you spend most of your time thinking about the past and very little time thinking about the future or living in the present. Someone living by this model feels depressed because most of their focus is always in the past and on things they cannot change or control. This model involves a lot of thinking and very little action.

Scenario two, the anxiety model, involves someone who spends a lot of time thinking about the future and divides the rest of their time thinking about the past or present. This person is very anxious, because instead of using the present to get things done, they are always worried about the next thing that is to come.

Finally, scenario three, the success model, involves someone using little time thinking about the past, some time thinking about the future, and most part of their time thinking about the present. This person looks back to what happened in the past and learns from it, looks to the future so they know the direction they want to go, and most important, spends most of their time in the present, getting things done. They know that they can't control the past and they can't control the future, but they can control what they do right now.

Meditation

Many books on happiness talk about the importance of meditation. Lately, I've been finding a lot of business and personal development books talking about this practice as well. Besides that, I've seen so many people meditating, especially successful people, that it made me think, why not try it? Contrary to what a lot of people think, meditation doesn't mean thinking about nothing, but learning how to focus and concentrate.

Our minds are receiving information all of the time and we end up getting overwhelmed. It's hard to concentrate, live in the present moment, or get what we need done, done. I've been going back and forth with this practice, and every time I feel anxious I have tried using a meditation app because it helps me retrain my brain to think about how I can better approach my situation.

My favorite ways to learn about meditation are through apps like Headspace or Insight Timer. The apps utilize guided meditation, which basically is someone guiding you through the meditation and giving you topics on which to think. I personally love Headspace, and I can't even tell you how relaxing and invigorating the meditations are. You can find packs for stress, happiness, relationships, and distractions. On the newer versions of Headspace, they also have features for sleeptime meditation as well as for workouts.

Don't care about what other people think

The "Man in the Arena" speech from Theodore Roosevelt changed my life when it came to others' perceptions of me. I first saw it in Brené Brown's Netflix special, called *The Call to Courage*. Honestly, it was one of the best things I've watched since *Friends*. In it, she talks about vulnerability and courage, but what stood out for me was this piece from "Man in the Arena":

"It is not the critic who counts; not the man who points out how the strong man stumbles, or where the doer of deeds could have done them better. The credit belongs to the man who is actually in the arena, whose face is marred by dust and sweat and blood; who strives valiantly; who errs, who comes short again and again [...]; who at the best knows in the end the triumph of high achievement, and who at the worst, if he fails, at least fails while daring greatly [...]."

As I have said before, this became the first page of many of my journals and it has changed my life. Brené also gave her own touch in the special that makes everything even more impactful. Here are a few things I learned:

- To be brave is a choice. Bravery is a choice you make every day when you get out of the bed. It's a choice that not everybody makes, therefore making it a choice that could set you apart from everybody else. Choose courage over comfort.
- If you choose to be brave, you are going to get your ass kicked. No matter what, you are going to fail and make mistakes. It's hard and it's painful. But it's always worth it and an inherent part of the process.

- "If you are not in the arena, you can't criticize my work." This is a big one for me, because I think a lot about what other people think of me. I have to take a step back and recognize that if they are not in the arena with me, if they are not doing what I am doing, they have no say in how I do it.
- People who love you are the best ones to give you feedback. They are the ones you need to care about. The people who love you truly want you to succeed. When feedback comes from them, you can listen and decide to accept it or not.
- What is winning? One more time we are talking about meaning. Maybe for you, winning is just showing up and being brave. You know what? That's more than a lot of people have ever done.

Comparing ourselves to one another is a survival instinct, and unfortunately we have a tendency to take it to the extreme. We want to do good and to be good and to belong to people; we certainly don't want to mess up or fail. However, nothing good comes from being safe. Choose to be brave, choose courage over comfort, and choose to be out there, setting an example for everybody. You might just get some people to join you.

You are the average of the people you most the spend time with

Have you ever heard that you are the average of the five people with whom you most spend time? Think about your closest friends and you will realize that you share the same ways of talking, dressing, and sometimes thinking. You might like the same kind of music, books, and TV shows. It's surprising to see how much you have in common with those you contact the most. Another thing we share with our close friends or family members is our emotions. If you are around people who are always complaining, you might be one of those people, too. If you are around people who are motivated, you will be, too.

The point here is that being around people who are happy and smart makes you happier and smarter as well. I've heard before that you should always be the least intelligent person at the table, because that way you can always learn something. When thinking about your goals and where you want to be in life, are you surrounded by the right people? I'm not telling you to get rid of your friends, but rather to look for more people who can influence and help you get closer to what you want.

By the way, you don't even need to go too far from your cell phone to do this. Reading good books, watching good content, or listening to good podcasts are all ways you can receive better input and feel closer to people who hold similar values and priorities as you.

Right now, take a look at your life and ask yourself what kind of influence you need, then go searching for that person. You are the average of the people you spend the most time with, so look for people who can push you up rather than pull you down.

> **Think about it**
> Go online right now and look for some books or pod-casts that you might find interesting. Test your theory for a couple of weeks and observe how your behavior and thinking processes might be changing. Choose people to learn from who are where you want to be, and learn as much as you can from them.

Learn how to accept your emotions

In his book, *The Happiness Trap*, Russ Harris tells a story about how to accept our emotions. He says that every time we are doing something that matters, we feel overwhelmed by a bunch of emotions that sometimes block us from getting what we want.

The analogy he uses is one where you are sailing a boat and trying to get closer to the shore. Every time the boat gets close to the shore, monsters come from below the deck and start moving in your direction. When the boat goes farther out to sea, the monsters go back to where they came from.

If you keep trying to get close to the shore, you will eventually realize that the monsters, although they are scary, don't attack, touch, or cause anyone any harm. The key to getting close to the shore is not to make the monsters go away, but to learn how to live with them, because they are always going to be there.

The same phenomenon occurs with our dreams. There is no way that our emotions are going away. Fear, anxiety, and stress are always going to be present; we just need to accept them and learn how to live with them. Don't see your emotions as a bad thing because you need to learn how to live with them. Don't suppress, don't hide. Just accept them, talk about them, and look for what the emotions are trying to tell you.

Fear, for example, is just trying to tell you to be more prepared. Fear was made to open your eyes, not to close them. Understand what you are feeling right now and evaluate it. Why did this emotion show up? What was your reaction? What could you have done better? Learn about your emotions and look for ways to cope with them. Before anything else, accept that your monsters will always be there, we just need to find a way to live with them.

The key is to being more conscious

The key to happiness is to be more conscious about it. The practices presented here are not hard to try, but they do require some level of attention and effort. You will see that, as with anything in life, when you start practicing them, they will become more familiar and easier. Eventually, without you even noticing, they will be part of your life and routine. As a consequence, you will also start feeling happier and more complete. Give them a try; what do you have to lose?

Takeaways

&—⚿ Happiness is something that you can and should start pursuing today. It's not about the past, it's not about the future, but it's about what is happening right now. "Happiness lost today is happiness for forever".

- Gratitude is important because it shifts our focus. We are so used to complaining and looking at what is wrong with life that we forget to look at things in a positive light. If we can look at the things we have and be grateful for them, our energy and focus will be on what makes us happy instead of what may be lacking.

- The key to being happier is to define happiness as something achievable that you can easily access.

- To feel happy, you need to either alter your expectations or work on bringing your life situation to meet the expectations you currently have.

- We should look back to what happened in the past and learn from it, look to the future so we know the direction we want to go, and most important, spend most of our time in the present, getting things done. We can't control the past and we can't control the future, but we can control what we do right now.

- Bravery is a choice you make every day when you get out of the bed. It's a choice that not everybody makes, therefore making it a choice that could set you apart from everybody else. Choose courage over comfort.

There is no way that our emotions are going away. Fear, anxiety, and stress are always going to be present; we just need to accept them and learn how to live with them.

CHAPTER 13

How Do I Know If It Will Work?

It will be all fine

One of my favorite stories about life is from Bruno Lima. I don't even know how to describe Bruno, other than by saying that he is one of the bravest people I know. After working for a big marketing company, he decided to start his own business. Long story short, he eventually felt like he wasn't happy in the business, so he sold it and moved to the northeast of Brazil to an amazing coastal city called Jericoacoara. He worked in a hostel for a few months as a way to escape and gather his thoughts.

When his time at the hostel was over, Bruno went back to his hometown and started another business selling ready-to-go fruits. A few months went by and the business didn't have the traction he was expecting. His venture had failed, and he left to go back to Jericoacoara. As if that wasn't enough, Bruno decided this time that he would hitchhike for more than 10 days, passing through beautiful places before getting to his final destination.

I was extremely impressed with this story, and I'd love for Bruno to write a book about it! Bruno is someone who was never afraid of failure. If things don't work out, he just moves onto the next challenge. I asked Bruno, "Knowing everything you know today, if you could go back in time and give yourself one piece of advice, what would you say?" He said, " I would tell myself everything will be okay." He said that people from the village in Jericoacoara used to say that a lot, and they never worried much about the tricks life can play. If they were out of gas, "it will be okay," if power went off, "it will be okay," no matter what happened, it would always be okay. Bruno now takes this philosophy and applies it to his life, and honestly, I think we all should. These days, Bruno runs a restaurant called Fruta na Casa (@frutanacasa) in his hometown, and is very happy.

We get so worried about life and don't take the time to understand the fact that honestly, everything will be okay. It always is. If we took the time we spend worrying about life to instead enjoy what it is giving us, we would get so much more out of our experience. There is never a way to predict what is going to happen, so we have to do the best with what we have and appreciate all life gives us.

What I love about Bruno's story is that he shows us to not be afraid of life. He is an example of what can happen when we have faith that things will be okay. If you are not happy about something in your life, make a change. It won't cost you anything, but it could show you something important about yourself. It's okay to take a break, it's okay to do something new that has nothing to do with your current position. No matter what, you just have to move forward and do something about your situation.

Sometimes Plan B works better than Plan A

One of the things that gives people a lot of anxiety is thinking about how life might go wrong at some point. People are worried that all that they have been doing—all the money, school, and time invested in that career or life will be thrown away if they choose something else. Then, they end up investing more time and effort into something that doesn't make them happy because they are afraid that they lost a bunch of time if they decide to move to a different life.

First, we need to understand that time is never wasted. We have to go through different experiences to get to know ourselves better and figure out who we are as people and professionals. The only way to get to know yourself — what you want to do, what you don't want to do, your values — is by throwing yourself into as many experiences as you can. Understanding the concept that you will never "waste" time may be a little hard, but it will help you to decrease your anxiety and frustration.

You will never waste your time because, always, always, always you will learn something from your experiences. It's only when you learn "who you are" — good or bad — and that failure and fear are part of the process of learning that you will truly understand... You will never waste your time.

I remember that a little before starting college, I had this perfect plan of how my life would play out. I started at 19 years old, and would be done school by 24 years old. Someone told me that I should get as many internships as possible during my time so I would be more "marketable" after graduation. After 24, I would get a good job in a big company and make my career there. I would get married at 28, have kids at 30, and after 10 years in the company, I would quit and open my own business.

Well, at the time of writing this book, I'm 28 and unmarried, I don't have and have not had a job in a big company and therefore never had an executive career. I opened my own business when I was 23 years old because of an amazing opportunity I had in the U.S. when I was 22 years old with the Leadership Development Program. We ran the business for about three years, and in the meantime I also worked as a consultant for small entrepreneurs for a year. I came to the U.S. in 2017 to get my MBA and work as the coordinator of the same program of which I had been a part. I worked with the LDP for three years, am now getting ready to start my PhD, and who knows what comes next.

My plans were never for any of this to happen, but my real life worked way better than my initial plan. I understand that plans are necessary because they give you a general direction, but they shouldn't take you to your final destination. We need plans because they gave us a sense of what to do next, but keep in mind that if your plans fall through, that doesn't mean you failed. Maybe something even better is about to come. You have to have certain experiences to get closer to the life you want.

Understanding that plan B might be better than plan A takes all the pressure off of things to happen exactly how you want them to happen. And, because you don't know how things would go prior to choosing a path, there is no way to predict the future of any plan. Whatever you chose, don't look back. Do and make the best from the path you chose, because that's the one you should've taken all along.

> **Think about it**
> Think about the twists you had in your life and reflect
> on how one little decision brought you to where you
> are right now. There is no way to predict if your life
> would've been different if you had taken a different path.
> Be grateful for where you are and soak up the best from
> wherever you go.

The truth is that you don't know

To be honest, maybe if my plan A had worked I would've
been happy with that also. Maybe I wouldn't have been. I
will never know, and that's okay. You don't know what would
have happened if you had chosen a different path. I know
people who have made a lot of money and are now ready to do
something to contribute to society. I know people who already
contributed to society and are now ready to make some money.
I know people who decided to focus on academics more than
the workforce. I know people who became entrepreneurs and
I know people who don't know anything yet.

There is no right path, there is no wrong path, there is
only your path. I know that you will do the best you can
with what you have. Don't compare your experience to the
experience of other people because we are all different. We all
have different backgrounds, different stories, different friends,
families, dreams, and emotions.

We all have different lives and we always will. So, no
matter which path you choose, don't look back. Just do the
best you can. If it doesn't work out, know that you can pivot
and try something new. I said it before and I will repeat it:

We don't regret the things we do, but we regret the things we didn't do. Always go for it.

Exercise - Future lifeline

This exercise will help you plan for the different things that might happen in your life. The idea of planning multiple different scenarios that you are happy with takes the pressure off of the one goal and path that *needs* to work out.

For this exercise, we will be exploring the different possibilities of where your life might take you. We will be exercising our creativity and future thinking. A few chapters ago, you created a list of goals you want to develop in different areas. Here you will have the opportunity to organize those goals into different possibilities on a timeline. It will be very similar to the exercise you did at the beginning of the book, but this time, you'll be thinking about the future.

The idea is to help you to understand that we have infinite options when thinking about the future. The truth is that you will survive no matter what. You will adapt and do the best with what you have because that's all you have. Exercising future thinking and thinking about possibilities helps us to be less stressed about the future, because we know that no matter what, everything will be just fine.

We will be planning three different scenarios. It's very important to understand that we are not planning the best plan, the so-so plan, and the worst case scenario plan. Rather, when making the three possibilities, you should be happy with all of the plans you create.

For the exercise, create three plans for the next five years. Think about how your personal life, career, education will look. Also, think about other fun things you want to do with your life, whether it be to run a marathon, travel to Indonesia, or learn a new language. For each scenario, write down why you would be okay if that scenario *actually happened*.

You can be as creative as you want with those plans. I've seen people drawing, doing bullet point lists, or using Excel for it. Personally, I love drawing, so I just made a timeline and created things that I wanted to happen over the years. It's great to see that no matter what, we will always have a good life and everything will be alright.

Takeaways

- We get so worried about life and don't take the time to understand the fact that honestly, everything will be okay

- First, we need to understand that time is never wasted. We have to go through different experiences to get to know ourselves better and figure out who we are as people and professionals.

- Understanding that plan B might be better than plan A takes all the pressure off of things to happen exactly how you want them to happen. And, because you don't know how things would go prior to choosing a path, there is no way to predict the future of any plan.

There is no right path, there is no wrong path, there is only your path. I know that you will do the best you can with what you have.

CHAPTER 14

Knowing Everything I Know Today

Your future is just like a block of wood

Your future is like a big block of wood, massive and solid. From this moment forward, you are an artist and your only tool is a chisel. Your job is to shape that piece of wood every day, little by little. It won't be easy and it will take a long time, but the more time you spend shaping it, the more beautiful and fascinating it will become. The key to making this masterpiece is patience in your work and in your choices.

Working on your future won't always be fun because things that matter in life are usually hard to get. Think about the time you invest into carving your block. Is it the same amount of time that you spend making choices about your future? It doesn't matter where you start, what matters is the work and time you put into creating your own brilliant future.

Don't worry if you don't know what you want the final result of your sculpture to look like. You may start carving a duck and, in the end, create a beautiful eagle (or vice versa!). The important thing is to begin carving the block of wood today, to start the process of making something beautiful.

What matters most are the choices you make in life. Every choice you make will lead you to a positive or negative experience, which will lead you to a life lesson. The person you will become is a direct consequence of the experiences you have lived. The more experiences you have, the more beautiful your wood block carving will be.

Therefore, only when you dedicate moments from your present life will you have a chance at a brilliant future. As soon as you begin to carve your block of wood that is your life, the beauty will begin to shine through your piece of art.

Knowing everything I know today...

Knowing everything I know today, if the person I am now could give my 18-year-old self advice, I would tell me to throw myself into as many experiences as I could, reflect about each one of them, and keep learning from all I can. I would tell myself to be calm and that everything will be okay, because it always is.

Experiences make us who we are. They are the best way to find out more about ourselves, what we like, and what we don't like. Talk to more people, get to know more places, make more mistakes, fail more, go on more adventures, read more books, learn more, and live more.

Reflect about everything you do. Carry your journal with you as much as you can and write things down. Clear the processes in your head so you can think about the direction you want to go next. Remember, if we spend 1% of our time reflecting about our lives, we can be much more fulfilled on the journey to reaching our dreams. Look up often toward where you are going before taking the next step in any direction.

Finally, keep learning from everything—the experiences, the people around you, books, podcasts, endless resources that you have at your fingertips. Be the least smart person at the table and never assume you know enough. There is always something we can learn about how to be better people or better professionals. Have a growth mindset and always look for the positive meanings in everything you do.

And please, don't rush. Take your time and enjoy the ride. Years ago, I was on a plane from São Paulo to Uberaba in Brazil. It's no surprise that turbulence happens on flights, but that flight in particular had way too much. When you've been travelling for a while, you understand that turbulence is just part of the process of flying and you end up getting used to it. In fact, I've even heard that it's very unlikely an airplane will crash due to turbulence.

On this particular flight, I decided to watch people during the turbulence. I saw people closing their eyes and holding onto the arm rests, I saw people praying and I saw people hugging whomever was with them. The thing is that if the airplane really did end up crashing, there wasn't anything any of us could do. No matter how much you hold onto the arm rests or the people around you, whatever is meant to happen will happen. Therefore, you have two choices: you either freak out or you enjoy the ride.

As it turns out, life is a little like that, too. Failure, mistakes, shame, and fear are always going to be present. They are part of the process of travelling through living life. You can do whatever you want in situations that make you uncomfortable, but you really only have two choices: you either freak out or you learn how to enjoy the ride.

This book was my way to help you choose to enjoy the ride. Don't rush life; take your time. Even though people think life is too short, we still have plenty of time to do all the things we want to do. The important things to remember are to always keep moving and to soak up the most that we can from our wonderful, wild, unforgettable, incredible lives.

Enjoy the ride.

Acknowledgements

I always thought it was very cliche when someone began their acknowledgements section by thanking their family. Of course you should be thanking them, especially your parents, the people who put you on the earth. But now that I am here, I realize I have so much more than just that for which to thank them. My family has taught me more than half of the things I have included in this book, but more importantly, they have taught me how to look at the world with positive eyes. Because of them, I know to never lose hope and to trust that in the end, everything will always be okay. My family taught me how to smile and the importance of being polite and kind to others. They taught me how to be persistent, loving, and caring. They've always shown me that I have to go after the things I dream about, and that if things don't work out they will always be ready to welcome me home. Thank you to my mom, Joceli, for being the most positive person I know. Thank you to my dad, Carlos, for working tirelessly and still making time to play with us kids. Finally, thank you to my brother, Henrique, for teaching me that hard work pays off, to constantly be persistent, and to go after the things that matter to me.

My family is my base, but many other people have contributed to making me the person I am today. Thank you Felipe Thomes and Jean Carvalho for believing in the Movement Journey dream, and for making it happen for as long as we could. Thank you Fabio Estrella, Rodrigo Bellini, Camila Cerezer, Gabriel Cardozo, Henrique Seixas (again), and João Pedro Achiles for being part of our team. Thank you to everybody who ever believed in the movement and hired us for a speech or training.

Thank you to the Leadership Development Program of SIUC, for introducing me to the leadership world and igniting this passion inside of me. Thank you to all my students over the years; you guys made everything so easy for me! Thanks also to everyone who ever joined my early experiments of the Dream Lab. You guys are amazing!

I also want to thank all my family for encouraging and supporting me, and all my friends from different spheres of life for always being there whether things were good or bad. I am who I am because of all of you. Thank you!

Lastly, I also want to thank you (the one with this book in your hands) for being here and believing in my dream. We are stronger and will go further together.

Don't forget to be awesome.

I'll see you soon ;)

Diogo Seixas

Resources

Below you will find a list of all the books and TED talks mentioned in this book.

Books

Awaken the Giant Within: How to Take Immediate Control of Your Mental, Emotional, Physical and Financial Destiny! by Tony Robbins

Built to Last: Successful Habits of Visionary Companies by James C. Collins

Business Model You: A One-Page Method For Reinventing Your Career by Alexander Osterwalder, Tim Clark, and Yves Pigneur

Creative Schools:The Grassroots Revolution That's Transforming Education by Ken Robinson

Designing Your Life: How to Build a Well-Lived, Joyful Life by Bill Burnett and Dave Evans

Dot Journaling—A Practical Guide: How to Start and Keep the Planner, To-Do List, and Diary That'll Actually Help You Get Your Life Together by Rachel Wilkerson Miller

Drive: The Surprising Truth About What Motivates Us by Daniel Pink

Essentialism: The Disciplined Pursuit of Less by Greg McKeown

Find Your Why: A Practical Guide for Discovering Purpose for You and Your Team by David Mead, Peter Docker, and Simon Sinek.

Good to Great: Why Some Companies Make the Leap... and Others Don't by James C. Collins

Great by Choice: Uncertainty, Chaos, and Luck--Why Some Thrive Despite Them All by James C. Collins

Happiness by Design: Finding Pleasure and Purpose in Everyday Life by Paul Dolan

"If You're So Smart, Why aren't You Happy?" by Raj Raghunathan.

Influence: The Psychology of Persuasion by Robert Cialdini

Mindset: The New Psychology of Success by Carol Dweck

O Poder da Ação by Paulo Vieira

Start with Why: How Great Leaders Inspire Everyone to Take Action by Simon Sinek

The Alchemist by Paulo Coelho

The Happiness Trap: Stop Struggling, Start Living by Russ Harris

The One World Schoolhouse: Education Reimagined by Salman Khan.

The Power of Habit: Why We Do What We Do in Life and Business by Charles Duhigg.

You, Your Child, and School: Navigate Your Way to the Best Education Ken Robinson

TED Talks

How great leaders inspire action by Simon Sinek

Inside the mind of a master procrastinator by Tim Urban

Why you will fail to have a great career by Larry Smith

Author Bio

Diogo is a dreamer by nature; he loves planning and strategizing about the future. He is also passionate and enthusiastic about learning and teaching. If you ever want to learn from life or about life, he is the best person to learn with. He is always finding analogies to describe the most important and common things everybody should know. From being lost once in life (or honestly, more than once) and finding himself, he now loves helping others who are in the same situation. He teaches them to gather their thoughts together in times of great uncertainty, especially students and young adults. This became a major part of his life when he founded his project, Journey Movement, which helped and developed over 4,000 people in the U.S. and Brazil. He also served as the coordinator of the Leadership Development Program of Southern Illinois University at Carbondale, where he helped over 100 students in between 2017 and 2020. Diogo has a graduate degree in Production Engineering from the Universidade Federal do Triângulo Mineiro in Brazil and an MBA from SIUC, where he is currently pursuing his PhD in Business Administration.

How to reach me

Website: https://www.rideacad.com/

Instagram: @ride.acad

LinkedIn: https://www.linkedin.com/in/diogoseixas/

Did You Like The Book?

I hope you really enjoyed your journey through these pages!

The experience of writing this book has been amazing, and it has been such a great personal accomplishment for me. If you think more people should read this book, here are a few things you can do:

- Leave a review on Amazon—this will help us get more people to see the lessons in this book.
- Share the book on Instagram and tag us: @ride.acad
- Tell your friends about the book, or, maybe just pass it on if you think someone could benefit from reading it.
- Check us out at https://www.rideacad.com/ for more content.

How Can I Do Better?

If there is anything you would like to have learned over the course of this book but didn't, please let me know! I promise I will work on it and either publish online, or, who knows, it will be in the next book ;)

To send feedback, you can go to https://www.rideacad. com/feedback or scan the QR code below: